Praise fo
Freedom to

T0151428

I was hooked on the book on the first page of the preface. Many readers will have a similar reaction, recognizing their own school experiences as students and teachers and seeing the wisdom of teaching children with these methods. Despite decades of new ideas and approaches to education, it all comes down to this—that which makes the greatest difference in schools fulfilling their mission is the nature of the teacher-child interaction, moment by moment, as the days and years unfold. All teachers and teachers-in-training should read this book and implement its strategies. Their students would benefit greatly.

—Dr. Stan Paine, former National Distinguished Principal
and Oregon Elementary Principal of the Year

Freedom to Learn is a methodology that will breathe the passion back into one of the most under appreciated professions. This book provides a comprehensive and flexible means of managing psychological and physical needs in children to motivate growth through effective learning. The much-needed ground work for a revolution of traditional classroom approaches that the children of coming generations deserve. A must read, must know, must teach.

—Dr. Dustin Marsh, Psy.D.

Freedom to Learn gripped me from the introduction all the way to the ending. This is a practical and useful book for seasoned teachers, beginning teachers, and students planning to become educators. Impressive, easy to read, practical, useful, creates a positive learning environment, and has data to support its effectiveness.

—Marlene Andrews, retired Faculty Member,
Special Education Department, University of Wisconsin Oshkos

Educators at all levels are beginning to pay much more attention to social-emotional learning, and the search for effective methods in that arena leads to Willans and Williams' work. After reading and studying *Freedom to Learn*, educators will understand the vital importance of the connection students must feel with peers, their surroundings, and especially with their teacher, for learning to occur. To make the concepts actionable, readers are introduced to difference-making strategies, which can be put in place immediately. *Freedom to Learn* is not your typical approach, but how well has the typical approach been working for either individual educators or for the entire educational system in our nation? In striving to develop lifelong learners, *Freedom to Learn* puts the why and the how-to together, clearly documenting the need to reject temporary test score improvement as validation of educational success. It is not just another educational philosophy book to read, but instead, it is a "must read and must implement".

—William J. Decker, Chief Administrator,
Mississippi Bend Area Education Agency

Freedom to Learn is one of those rare books which can be utilized as a training tool in the educational discipline. It holds the wisest, most reasonable, and compassionate treatment for every student. The authors exude passion as they provide practical strategies for educators, which will develop a trusting relationship with each student; affording all students' success. As an educator, counselor, private therapist and professor at the university level for more than forty years, I avidly recommend *Freedom to Learn* for every current educator as well as those working toward an educational career.

—Karen M. Smith, M.Ed., Ed.S., National Certified School Counselor

freedom *TO* learn

Creating a Classroom
Where Every Child Thrives

WILLANS & WILLIAMS

new society
PUBLISHERS

Inquiries regarding requests to reprint all or part of *Freedom to Learn* should be addressed to New Society Publishers at the address below. To order directly from the publishers, please call toll-free (North America) 1-800-567-6772, or order online at www.newsociety.com

Any other inquiries can be directed by mail to:
New Society Publishers
P.O. Box 189, Gabriola Island, BC V0R 1X0, Canada
(250) 247-9737

LIBRARY AND ARCHIVES CANADA CATALOGUING IN PUBLICATION

Willans, Art, 1943-, author
        Freedom to learn : creating a classroom where every child thrives
/ Willans & Williams.

Includes bibliographical references and index.
Issued in print and electronic formats.
ISBN 978-0-86571-878-4 (softcover).--ISBN 978-1-55092-671-2 (PDF).--
ISBN 978-1-77142-266-6 (EPUB)

        1. Classroom management. 2. Classroom environment. 3. Effective
teaching. 4. Problem children--Education. I. Williams, Cari Lynette, author
II. Title.

LB3013.W48 2018   371.102'4   C2017-907285-4
                                            C2017-907286-2

Funded by the Government of Canada | Financé par le gouvernement du Canada

 Canada

New Society Publishers' mission is to publish books that contribute in fundamental ways to building an ecologically sustainable and just society, and to do so with the least possible impact on the environment, in a manner that models this vision.

MIX
Paper from responsible sources
FSC
www.fsc.org   FSC® C016245

Certified
B Corporation

new society
PUBLISHERS

Contents

Preface

M Y FIRST MEMORY OF SCHOOL was not a good one. It was a really important day in kindergarten, because it was the first time we were going to use scissors. I was so excited to show I would be the best student ever to use a pair of scissors. This was my chance to prove that I could remember everything my teacher had said. She had taught us never to cut our hair or the hair of other students. We were to be careful never to cut our clothes, and most of all never run with scissors. I was certain I could not only remember everything she had said, but would follow her instructions exactly. The moment I was waiting for finally arrived. She said, "Children you may come get your scissors." In my excitement to show her I could be a perfect student, I jumped to my feet and ran to the box of scissors. I successfully knocked three of my classmates out of the way and grabbed a pair. With perfect discipline, I calmly turned around to walk to my seat. The teacher was yelling my name, which surely meant she was as pleased with me as I was with myself. To my heart-breaking surprise, she was upset with me and took my most cherished possession — the scissors — from my hand. She said, "Cari, you are not allowed to use scissors." Because of the way she said those words, I thought she meant "forever." My spirit was broken. In my mind, I was a miserable failure as a student and would have to come to school every day for the rest of my life and bear the shame of being a failure. All of my friends, if I ever had any more friends, would know me as the girl who could not use scissors.

Despite how impossible survival seemed, I did make it to the fifth grade. My fifth grade teacher, Mrs. Cynthia Lowery, made all the difference in my life and in the lives of other students. She made the classroom safe. The students, including myself, were never afraid of failing or even disappointing her. Every student succeeded and we became part of the fifth grade family that kept each other safe. She loved each of us, including the most difficult boy in the class. Every student became committed to helping that boy succeed. For years, I and a few other students remained in contact with her, and I babysat her children. Even though Cynthia is the reason I became a teacher I couldn't describe what it was about her teaching that made such a difference. However, I knew I wanted my students to respond the way we responded to Cynthia. But while I knew how I wanted students to respond, I did not know how to achieve those results.

While pursuing my dream as an education major at the University of Nevada, I looked for a position that would allow me to gain some classroom experience. My first job interview took me to A Child's World where I met Dr. Willans (Art) who interviewed me for a preschool teaching position. During the interview he said, "Describe for me how you want the students in your classes to respond."

I said, "Until yesterday I would have known exactly how to respond to that question. However, yesterday a teacher told me that I was way too idealistic. She explained that my expectations of students were impossible, and I would quickly become disillusioned with teaching."

Art responded, "I would like to hear your idealistic description of what you want your classroom to be like and how you developed your ideas." One day earlier I would have had incredible confidence in answering that question. However, I remember having to screw up my courage to describe my apparently foolish ideas. I began by saying, "I was afraid of failing for my first five years of school. However, in the fifth grade I had a teacher who made it easy and rewarding to learn. The class was more like a big family than a classroom. I don't understand all the techniques she used to help us grow, but I am hoping to learn them before I become a certified teacher." Art had a pleasant look on his face and expressed his interest in what I had to say by nodding his approval. I continued, "I don't want students to be afraid of making mistakes; they should gain the courage to try, to do, and to consider mistakes as a painless part of learning." Art waited for me to continue. I added, "I want students to learn more than any teacher could ever teach. I don't yet know how to make that happen, but if I remember right, my fifth grade teacher did all of that and more. Maybe someday I should look her up and get her to tell me how."

Thinking I had answered his question, I paused. He said, "Go on."

I remember thinking, "What kind of interview is this? How extensive do my answers have to be?" However, the kindness in his voice helped me gather more courage to continue. I explained, "In that fifth grade class, Cynthia never had to be mean, because we just cooperated with how she expected us to act. I remember one student, who gave her more trouble than the other students. Nevertheless, she maintained her patience with him and it seems to me he did better by the end of the year. I think the most important thing I remember is that I, and I think other students, developed the confidence that we could succeed at anything. Do you want me to go on?"

"I have heard enough," Art answered. Before he could continue my heart stopped. I was sure he was going tell me that such expectations were impossible. He continued, "I have heard enough to know that your fifth grade teacher represented what we want all teachers to accomplish. Not many teachers come to us with a well-formed idea of how students should respond to being in school. The ultimate goal of education is not only developmental and academic accomplishments, but what kind of people our students will become."

To conclude the interview, he described many methods necessary to accomplish my goals. He further explained that my performance as a teacher would be evaluated on my use of those methods. I was not scared of these demands, but instead became enthusiastic. He had not said that my ideas were unrealistic, but instead validated my ideas and described how I could accomplish my goals.

1

Students Reaching Their Potential

Mrs. Jill Moningham, a primary grade coordinator, paused for a moment outside Sunrise Elementary school, which for several years had been designated as needing to improve the academic success of its students. The school sat in an area of a mid-sized city where few students had ever received any pre-K preparation. Most of the families had few if any books for their children and academic attainments fell below expected standards year after year. On this bright, sunny, warm day in May, Jill proceeded to her office to gather the materials she would need to continue to oversee the end-of-year testing. Her principal, Mrs. Donaldson, had appointed her to monitor all the school's testing to maintain the integrity of the process. Throughout the process she had noted, as she had in previous years, the anxiety of most students and many teachers. However, a week earlier she noted an exception. The students in Laura Gilmore's second grade class were confident, composed, and looking forward to showing how much they had learned. That difference caught her attention, but the results were even more remarkable. Laura's second grade class had outscored every other class in the school. The school evaluated all students in reading, math, and writing with percentile ranks assigned to every student. At the beginning of the year all of the second grade students had scored at or below the 50th percentile. In fact, the average percentile score for the school was 37 and the average score for second graders was the 34th percentile. Laura's class in particular had averaged at the 32th percentile at the beginning of the year. When all the testing was done and scores recorded, school wide the scores had improved slightly, but again had fallen short of the goals set by the new principal. However, in Laura's class, 96 percent of the students had exceeded the 65th percentile. The average percentile rank in her class was 83. Throughout the school, including the other second grade classes, only a few classes had half their students score above the 50th percentile.

The teacher, Laura, was new to the school that year. Mrs. Donaldson, the principal, knew her from before and had encouraged her to apply when the position opened. Jill wondered if some difference in teaching accounted for the better academic results. However, since the school year was coming to a close she would have to act fast to find the answer. First she looked back to previous years and found that in her previous schools, Laura's classes had consistently out-performed other classes. These differences begged the question: was Laura that much better at teaching than the others?

Once the testing was complete, Jill Moningham made time and conducted observations of many teachers, including Laura. She found no difference in how dedicated the teachers were. Nearly all the teachers were dedicated professionals who worked hard and wanted the best for their students. Was this one teacher using some special technique that could result in such differences? While that question proved more difficult to answer, nothing stood out as a special teaching strategy. Was this teacher somehow doing everything better than the other teachers? That was not so either.

In fact, it turned out Laura was doing many things very differently than other teachers. Jill found that nearly all of the other teachers were conscientiously using standard methods. They were teaching the way they learned to teach, following the recommended guidelines from both district and school administrators. She did not have to study the broader picture, she knew the teaching methods in their district were widely recommended throughout the country. However, in that one second grade classroom where the students had done so much better, some aspects of the teaching process were very different from what other teachers were doing. As Jill pursued this difference, she found some teachers felt that Laura did not do some things the recommended way, but somehow it always worked out for her. Her students always excelled and she never had major behavior problems.

Jill could have dismissed the whole thing as inexplicable. To her credit she did not do that. She believed, or at least strongly suspected, that the success was dependent on the teaching process. She approached Laura and struck up a conversation.

"I notice your students did very well on end of year evaluations," she said.

"Thank you. I was pleased with how they did," Laura responded.

"I took the liberty to look back and found that your results have been very good for all of the 14 years you have taught."

"Yes, that's true."

Jill explained, "I'm trying to figure out why that is."

"I think it is because of the way I teach."

"But I notice you don't use many of the standard methods we recommend," Jill continued.

Laura acknowledged that to be true: "Every method I use, and don't use, is purposeful. Everything I say to every student is designed to help them become more successful."

"It seems like you got lucky and didn't have any students with behavior problems this year."

At this point Laura reminded her that through the year the principal had moved several difficult students into her class. In fact, two of those students had caused so much disruption in their original class they had made learning impossible. Jill acknowledged that she remembered how difficult those students had been.

Laura explained, "My teaching methods reduce the behavioral issues by increasing cooperation and creating a desire to succeed."

"But when I observed your class, I didn't see any procedures directed at reducing behavioral problems," Jill replied.

"On the contrary, I use methods designed to help children learn to behave so they can excel at learning."

"I'm afraid I don't understand," Jill answered.

"I can't explain it in ten minutes or even an hour. But I have been using these techniques for nearly 20 years, and my results are always the same." (The 20 years included her experience in preschool and special education.)

Laura continued, "Despite which students are in my class they always succeed. I think what you are seeing in other classes are procedures designed to intervene when problem behavior occurs. In contrast, I direct nearly all of my attention to developing students into better learners. I have to get to class now, but maybe we could talk later."

After more than a decade of the 21st century, only a little more than a third of all eighth grade students in this country are proficient in reading and math. This represents a major failure of education and problem for society and has not been solved by increasing school budgets, teacher training, or putting more pressure on teachers. Some schools, with the blessing of state and federal bureaucrats, have attempted to address the problem with policy changes including smaller class sizes and more frequent testing of students. Some of those may have helped a bit, but national test data suggests none have had a major impact on academic performance. Many observers have blamed society, parents, or students themselves. However, placing blame cannot and will not help students achieve academic excellence. After careful consideration, we believe the only solution for advancing all students to academic proficiency is to adopt new methods of teaching. New methods in a couple of classrooms in a few schools will not solve the enormous problem facing our country. Pressuring teachers to do better with current methodologies will frustrate teachers but will not solve the problems. Finding effective methods of producing academic excellence is essential.

The conversation continued a few days later.

Jill asked, "What are the most important parts of your teaching methods?"

Laura responded, "I want my students to take as much responsibility for their own learning as I take for teaching. From the first day, I am developing all students as effective learners. No benefit can come from expecting students to learn until they learn how to learn and help each other learn. My methods must enhance the personal and academic development of all students. Also, I have to get them to work together and help each other. The bridge they have to cross is very wide, so the only thing they can do is to grow a little bit every day."

"But I still don't understand how you get all the material to them."

Laura explained, "Teaching must be about getting students to learn and take responsibility for learning. Imparting knowledge is a small, easy part of it. The hard part is getting 25 students to work together as a team."

"Well, I don't see how any other teacher could, if necessary, step in and teach your class," Jill responded.

"Remember, when I was gone on family business for a week in March? These students did beautifully for the substitute."

"Yes, now that you mention it, I do remember that," said Jill.

Laura further explained, "The students had learned how to behave. They were not behaving to impress me, but behaving to benefit themselves and each other."

"I must admit, you have had success with some difficult students. But I still don't think it will work with all students," Jill argued.

"Of course it works with all students. The entire concept is built on the science of human behavior and neuropsychology. If implemented correctly, it can't fail any more than an apple can fall toward the sky."

"It all sounds good, but I can't train other teachers to teach the way you teach," Jill complained.

Laura said, "On the contrary, I was trained more than 20 years ago while teaching in a preschool. It took me just a few days to see results and less than six months to become proficient at the process."

"We can't all go back to teaching preschool to learn what you learned."

Laura further explained, "The man I learned from has trained teachers from preschool through eighth grade. He has trained regular teachers and special education teachers. He has worked in suburban schools, inner city schools, and even in schools integrated with treatment programs for children with behavioral and emotional disorders."

"Who is this guy?" Jill asked.

"Dr. Art Willans. In fact, he is collaborating on a book for elementary teachers with a teacher in Reno. That is where his program is located."

Mrs. Moningham said, "I would like to meet him."

A Small Beginning for New Methods

For someone to understand Art, they must understand how determined he is to find ways to help children. He never accepts that a child cannot learn. Perhaps that characteristic is best illustrated by a story from his early years as a professional. Many years ago and before receiving his doctorate, he got a request from a preschool to help with a four-year-old nonverbal boy. Most people who knew the boy assumed he was seriously disabled intellectually, which was plausible because his mother had an intellectual disability. In his four years, the boy had said only two words. He did not run or play. If handed a toy, he would look at it momentarily and lay it down, but reportedly had never picked one up on his own. Even though he could not use a spoon or fork, he could drink from a baby cup and feed himself when provided finger foods. The preschool personnel hoped Mr. Willans could teach the boy to say and understand a few words. Art researched the recommended methods for addressing the issues.

For the first session he scheduled a room in the church that housed the preschool. At first he made no progress, but Art refused to accept that the boy could not learn and soon abandoned the widely accepted methods recommended in the literature. He concluded that to help this boy, he would need entirely different methods. At that point he had less confidence in his intuition, but believed that if he could get the methods right the boy would learn. After formulating a new plan he immediately got to work. In just three days the boy said his third word — truck — which he repeated hundreds of times that day. Within two weeks he was beginning to participate in preschool activities. These intuitive methods that were not described in the literature proved effective. Art wanted the boy to see, touch, and hear everything possible while Art described it all in simple language. The boy learned to talk, play, and participate in activities alongside his classmates. His preschool teachers soon learned the methods. In just a few weeks, they discovered the boy was intellectually gifted, not disabled. Soon the one-on-one process gave way to a very early version of the group process described in this book. Despite his mother's intellectual disability and their impoverished living conditions, many years later the boy graduated from high school with honors. Art could have accepted the ready-made excuse that the boy could not learn like other students. The accepted methods of the time, which were not that much different from the accepted methods now, would have fulfilled everyone's prophecy. However, he found new methods and averted a tragedy. Art still subscribes to the philosophy that when teachers get the methods right, students will learn.

A few years later, Art commenced work on his doctorate. His professor shared his belief that given the correct methods, students will learn. This philosophy has the inherent advantage of never allowing excuses. Poverty, lack of parent involvement, disabilities, budget cuts, inadequate classrooms, behavior problems, students with mental health problems, and administrators who are not supportive, cannot prevent student success. The only issue that prevents students' success is the ineffective methods provided to teachers. Over the last 20 years, the authors have repeatedly proven that every student can excel. Universally effective methods mean that every teacher can be successful.

We want to clarify: when we describe the accomplishments all students can make, we are referring to regular elementary education classrooms. We do not have similar verified data from special education classrooms; however, the methods would apply and be effective in most special education programs. We have known teachers who have successfully used some parts of this methodology with various special populations. However, we do not have access to any actual results of academic accomplishments from such classrooms. Differences would be inevitable, because results comparable to what we are reporting could not be attained with students with severe intellectual disabilities or a deaf/blind population. While Art did, at one time, work with a deaf/blind population, he did not use this methodology with that group. Currently, Art is serving preschool children with severe behavioral and emotional difficulties. He is using all of the methods described in this book, but those results and variations in the application are beyond the scope of the current book. Because many students are failing to reach grade level criteria, this book is dedicated to promoting methods that can help regular schools.

Like Laura, Cari learned Art's methodology from him years ago. Most of the time since then the authors have worked separately, but both have had remarkable results. This book is dedicated to describing the methods necessary to make academic accomplishment possible for elementary students. Because most of the verifiable results achieved by

Dr. Willans have been in an early childhood mental health program, we will focus on the results Mrs. Williams has achieved in elementary schools. For most of her career, she has taught in Title 1 or underperforming schools. (To qualify as a Title 1 school, the school must have a large concentration of students from low income families.) However, in her classes, every student makes excellent academic progress. Good-to-excellent progress is common in many suburban schools throughout this country. A man both of us respect greatly once explained that without knowing anything about a community, he could fly over a city and pick out the highest performing schools. His point was that a very high correlation would exist between the best schools and the better socioeconomic areas that could be identified from the air.

While we could not disagree with the correlation, this does not explain how every year Cari gets results comparable to the best schools in the state. When such results do occur, they may be ignored. Educators and bureaucrats frequently miss the solution because their attention is directed to fixing what is wrong, instead of replicating what is right. Because the same students are failing every year with different teachers, the problem appears to be outside the control of schools. Educators may disregard isolated success because they do not recognize it being related to teaching methods. Because educators can do nothing to change the socioeconomic areas of a city, the unfortunate, but misguided, conclusion is that little can be done to effect change in underperforming schools.

Working in the shadow of systemic excuses, some teachers do face an uphill battle. Fortunately, many administrators have refused to accept defeat, and have spent considerable amounts of money and directed resources to find solutions. Unfortunately, most efforts have at best produced modest gains as measured by academic achievement. We have found that many of the typical methods described in hundreds of books hinder successful learning. This lack of success using standard methods has caused much blame to be directed at teachers, parents, students, administrators, and schools. As a result, effective solutions have not been found. Despite all efforts the same students continue to fail and the same schools continue to underperform. Unless a new perspective can resolve the issue, the conclusion that the problem lies with the students and/or their parents is likely to continue. Fortunately, this book not only provides that perspective but precisely describes the exact process necessary for every school to be successful. With small changes in teaching methodology, students in our best schools could do even better than they are now and students in Title 1 schools would make outstanding progress. Administrators do not have to settle for teachers struggling to maintain order and failing to educate many students. The alternative is to give teachers methods that will promote cooperation and develop students who are self-driven to excel. Meeting academic standards is within the reach of every student.

Most educators link academic problems in our schools to classroom behavior. Without a doubt, behavioral issues in many schools consume too much time and adversely affect achievement. Teachers, administrators, counselors, and parents all become engulfed in attempting to solve a stream of behavioral problems. Many teachers spend an hour or more per day on behavior issues, and many principals average an hour per week per teacher on them. When teachers master the teaching process we will describe, principals will find they are spending much less time on behavioral problems. For instance, for Cari the cumulative number of hours in the last ten years that a principal or other professional has spent in response to a behavior issue in her class is zero. Perhaps readers should take an extra moment to consider the previous sentence. In ten years of teaching, in underperforming and Title 1 schools, she has handled every behavioral event internally. Furthermore, in ten years of teaching she has never convened an Individual Educational Plan (IEP) for a behavioral issue. The point is not that she has some magical way with students. The difference is nothing more than the methods she is using.

Good behavior is not for the convenience of the teacher. Students must behave appropriately to maximize learning. Success in school is in part dependent on appropriate conduct behavior, but teachers must accomplish their goal without impeding academic accomplishments. With the use of the methods we will describe, students begin the school year working on both developing appropriate conduct and mastering their academic assignments. Nevertheless, even during those few weeks, more learning will occur than is evident in other classrooms. In just a few weeks, as students learn to work together, the time spent on academics will exceed most other classes. Because students are behaving cooperatively, they quickly develop the behaviors necessary to become effective learners, and academic accomplishments soon follow.

In her career, Cari has shown how much students can achieve. Besides excellent conduct behavior, year after year in Title 1 schools her students excel academically. We will examine the current school year, 2016, in particular. For instance, the Developmental Reading Assessment (DRA) is scaled so that the expected level at the end of kindergarten is a score of three. However, the district in which she was teaching had arbitrarily set an expected level of four. In a typical school, educators would expect less than 40 percent of the students to reach or exceed a criterion increased by 33 percent. Given that she was teaching in a Title 1 school, the expectation would be for less than one third of the students to reach or exceed an elevated criterion. However, 85 percent of her kindergarten students met or exceeded level four in reading. The same 85 percent scored at or above criteria in math. Two of the three students who did not meet criteria joined the class in the second semester. Also, those two students reached the national criteria of three, but missed by one point meeting the arbitrary criteria. In a Title 1 school, 95 percent of her students met or exceeded national criteria in reading and math., Students have achieved similar results in Cari's classes every year. District administrators have said her results are comparable to those students from the best schools in the district. Recently an administrator said that she had blown away district averages. Students in Title 1 and underperforming schools can attain academic accomplishments like these every year.

We have seen enough instances in various programs to conclude that all students served in classrooms using these methods will attain — or even far exceed — grade level criteria. Many students can reach levels that suggest they are achieving to the limits of their potential. Psychologists call this "actualization." However, the term has always been used to describe adults who have apparently reached the limits that could be expected. Students in elementary school who have scored exceedingly well on achievement tests have not reached the limits they can achieve in adulthood. We have, therefore, coined the term, "developmental actualization" to refer to accomplishments that evidently are as good as could be expected, given the age and development of the individual. The point is that we have watched with amazement as students have attained unbelievable success. We have struggled to explain to parents and other professionals how students, who came from a home of barely functioning adults, could outscore the students from the most elite schools in the state. We were never satisfied with our description of what we were seeing until we came up with the new term.

One does not have to wait ten years to identify good teaching. Once a teacher is using effective methods, her skills and the resulting progress of students can immediately be recognized. For instance, Cari was identified as having excellent skills 20 years ago. In 1996, Art had a consultant friend, Dr. Stan Paine from Oregon, come in and evaluate his teachers. This consultant, who had been named elementary principal of the year in Oregon, considered Cari an outstanding teacher. He recognized the skills she used and the success she was having with students. She has improved her use of the methods every year since. Continuous improvement over several years is typical of many teachers using these methods. While Art developed much of the methodology we describe, Cari should get credit for showing how every student can achieve developmental actualization.

When a teacher in a Title 1 school can repeatedly get such results with virtually every student assigned to her, the only reasonable conclusion is that something is happening that cannot be ignored. Every district in the United States has a moral responsibility to replicate these methods. When teachers get it right, the results will follow. Unfortunately, observers in many outstanding classrooms are unable to recognize what they are seeing. Jill saw no behavior problems and noticed the teacher was not using standard procedures for dealing with inappropriate behavior; therefore, she assumed Laura had gotten all the best students. She failed to recognize that all students had learned to behave appropriately during the first three weeks of the school year. Very few educators would believe that with the appropriate methods, all students can learn and maintain appropriate behavior throughout the school year. Nevertheless, that is exactly what Laura had accomplished. Had she used standard methods, establishing the cooperative behavior would have been more difficult and maintaining such behavior would have been impossible. To most observers, including Jill, the differences are not always perfectly obvious. When observers notice good behavior, they think it might be the students or the timing. All students behave themselves sometimes. In Laura's class, observers might have noticed a few more positive interactions, but they could assume that to be correlated with having better kids. They might miss recognizing that different teaching methods were responsible for the better behavior. Unless an observer specifically knows what he is looking for, like the principal from Oregon, the teaching methods might seem like typical methods. However, readers should understand that a process that is so easily overlooked, is still easy for teachers to learn.

A review of data from public schools across this country reveals that students in some schools are achieving academic success. Unfortunately, it is also true that many students in our nation's schools are not being successful either from an academic or behavioral perspective. We will address this problem and show that every student, served in regular education classrooms, can meet or exceed grade level proficiency. In fact, with these methods schools could serve nearly all students in regular education classrooms. The teaching process we describe has proven successful with virtually every student from preschool through eighth grade. Art has successfully trained hundreds of teachers who have ranged from having a high school diploma to graduate degrees. Besides typical students, these teachers have served students with learning disabilities, behavior disorders, mental health issues, and many types of special needs.

This is not a dream of what schools will be like a thousand years from now. Teachers can produce these changes in just a few weeks. Success in classrooms does not need to be dependent on which students are assigned to the class. A teacher's career, or her happiness, is not dependent on getting promoted to a suburban school. Success can be completely dependent on the methods a teacher uses. The book you are holding contains the answer. When we talk to teachers, we suggest they envision how they want their students to behave and what they want them to learn. They always have ambitious ideas for their students. This book describes how they can realize those dreams and get the best from students.

We will end this chapter by explaining how this book will take readers on a journey describing a set of unique methods that teachers have never heard of, or seldom used. Readers will also find that while some aspects of behavioral science have been described perfectly throughout the educational literature, other aspects have been misrepresented and therefore misused. Some important findings of behavioral science, for instance, classical conditioning, have been considered irrelevant to teachers, but actually describe much of what is happening in classrooms. This book will, in simple language, describe some aspects of neuropsychology which in recent years have been the basis of books on social and emotional learning. However, our readers will further learn how neuropsychology explains why some students do not respond favorably to many standard classroom procedures and how teachers can use the current methods to be successful with every student. Teachers almost always work with a group of students and are too often expected to do so with little or no understanding of the dynamics of groups. For these reasons, readers will have to let the unique nature of our methods, and the surprising reasons behind them, unfold as they read. We think you will enjoy the journey and discover why Jill could not recognize the process Laura tried to describe to her.

Summary

- When the correct methods are used, students will learn.
- Fortunately, the methods are universal. All students respond to the same methods.
- The methods described later in this book will solve both behavioral and academic problems.
- Even with disadvantaged students behavioral and academic results will be higher than most educators have ever seen.
- Every year students evidently achieve near the limits of their potential. To describe that phenomenon, we coined the term developmental actualization.
- These methods are within the capabilities of every teacher.

2

Understanding Human Behavior

To EXPLAIN BOTH OUR METHODS and student behavior, we must first describe some factors of being human. Human behavior is driven by two types of needs: survival and psychological. First we will describe survival needs and the importance, for teachers, of one in particular. These include food, water, sleep, warmth, air, and body movement. In fact in this country, families and social programs largely assure children's survival. Only the need to move requires much of an explanation.

Readers will find it easy to understand how the need to move is important to animals that need to catch food and avoid predators. However, the need to move is still important for human survival. In fact, we evolved to stay in nearly constant motion except during periods of sleep. In order to avoid predators, early humans constantly moved from place to place as they hunted and gathered food. This had the added benefit of their scent not giving away their position. However, even in modern times, the importance of staying in constant motion becomes apparent in the following example. An unexpected blizzard caught an adolescent boy 12 miles from home. Few opportunities for shelter were available on the Midwestern prairie. The boy trudged nearly 11 hours through the rapidly accumulating snow. If that had been the first time he ever stayed in motion for an extended period, he would have perished. This boy quickly learned to conserve his energy, take short breaks to rest a minute or two, and think carefully about how best to survive. Those were the lessons dictated by the circumstances. Because staying alive was dependent on staying in constant motion, humans evolved to learn while in constant motion.

As inconvenient as it might be for teachers, that attribute of children has not changed in thousands of years and will not change for thousands more. To help students pursue learning in schools, teachers must have effective ways to deal with the need to move. Unfortunately for teachers, the requirements of modern education cannot be attained while students are in constant motion; therefore, we promote methods to help students voluntarily inhibit the need to move. Nevertheless, we are proponents of using movement in lessons, and many teachers are very good at incorporating movement into their lessons.

For students to excel in school, they must learn to suppress the natural tendency to be in constant motion. Those students who can limit their movement may succeed in school and those who cannot may be labeled hyperactive. Teachers may choose to use consequences for students who get out of their seats. Unfortunately, many standard techniques result in some students resenting school; as a result, they impede learning. Effective methods must enhance learning not impede it. The methods we recommend will not only be effective in getting students voluntarily to inhibit their need to stay in motion for several hours per day, but will simultaneously prepare the prefrontal cortex for learning. We will also describe the science behind these methods. With the appropriate teaching methods, about 90 percent of those students currently identified as hyperactive can not only learn to suppress their urge to move without medication, but at the same time develop more confidence to learn.

Humans also have psychological needs. These include the need for intellectual and sensory stimulation, autonomy/empowerment, avoiding or stopping pain, socialization, and the need for sex. While stopping physical pain could be a survival need, we will discuss it here because teachers deal mostly with psychological pain. Many teachers will notice that this list of needs resembles the hierarchy of needs described by Maslow. We deviate from Maslow's list, however, to structure our description to be more useful to teachers.

Curiosity, or the need for intellectual stimulation, accounts for much of mankind's advancement. Because schools exist to promote intellectual learning, educators often take for granted that children want to learn academic material. However, a student could just as easily satisfy this need on the streets, in a forest, or while surfing. People satisfy this need wherever they pursue activities. Many activities have the advantage of satisfying the need for intellectual stimulation while the person is in constant motion. Because the need does not discriminate between activities of great or little value in adult life, schools need methods that turn the reality of this need into a major advantage for teachers. The satisfaction of human needs is a natural and powerful motivator; therefore, those behaviors that result in need satisfaction are readily learned and voluntarily maintained.

Sensory perception is also a powerful motivator of human behavior. Many teachers create wonderful lessons around sensory experiences. These can provide excellent breaks from monotonous seatwork and benefit students. Some teachers use sensory activities as a reinforcer for a student to complete his work. Whereas the process may serve to reinforce the completion of work, the more important and often missed issue is that students must satisfy their needs while continuing to work.

Humans also have a need to avoid pain. Everyone understands physical pain associated with accidents, illness, and corporal punishment. However, humans can also feel psychological pain that is not as well understood, but is extremely important. If we could not feel psychological pain, we would also be incapable of joy, happiness, love, and other pleasant emotions. Because psychological pain is not very well understood, educators often disregard its effect on students. Too often in this culture, parents and even educators have ignored that children feel shame, guilt, become embarrassed, or are apprehensive about what adults will do to them. Whereas shaming or other forms of psychological pain will affect behavior, how they will change it is not predictable and seldom has the desired effect. Students experience far more psychological pain in classrooms than most teachers realize. Once a student experiences psychological pain, the task of getting the student back to an emotional state where he can learn is formidable. Students encountering psychological pain in classrooms will have increased anxiety, less trust of the teacher, and a reduced confidence in learning. In classrooms, psychological pain not only adversely affects the students' ability to learn, but also increases their need to move.

The innate response to anxiety is to move or get out of the situation. Humans survived for thousands of years because they avoided or moved away from situations that produced anxiety. Observations in Art's program over the past 25 years confirm that anxiety can produce a physiologically based motivation to stay in motion. In schools, students have virtually no way to escape; therefore, students may rely on another lesson learned thousands of years ago: when humans had no way to escape, they became fearful and learned to fight. When classrooms produce anxiety, students will stay in constant motion or become fearful and aggressive. This reaction is not what teachers have in mind when they use interventions that unintentionally elicit anxiety.

A second and even more destructive phenomena occurs when students experience psychological pain. A classical conditioning effect is unavoidable. For those who are unfamiliar with classical conditioning, the idea is better known as Pavlovian conditioning. Ivan Pavlov, the Russian physiologist and Nobel laureate, conditioned dogs to salivate when they heard a bell. Similarly, the anxiety or psychological pain that occurs in classrooms will result in students experiencing a conditioned anxiety response to teachers, schools, classrooms, and anything in the classroom. This issue brings the use of all negative stimuli in schools into question.

Fortunately, the opposite can also be true. When teachers create classrooms where their students trust them to prevent pain, students will respond differently. They will love going to school. Often Art has served children who had previously refused to go to school. However, upon enrollment in his program they could not be kept away.

Another psychological need, autonomy, is perhaps even less understood than psychological pain. If humans did not need autonomy, life could never have continued past the first generation. All creatures, including children, must learn to take care of themselves, or even protect themselves to survive. Even as early as the toddler years, children realize that to some extent they can take care of themselves and do not need to rely on adults for everything. As early as six months, children begin to do a few things for themselves. However, they remain almost totally dependent on adults. One of the difficulties facing parents and teachers is that they must gradually allow for more and more autonomy. In fact, the need for autonomy is evident whenever children want to do things for themselves. Whereas a toddler is highly dependent on adults for her survival, children become less and less dependent on adults as they mature. Because the need for autonomy changes throughout life, teachers must understand how to promote responsible autonomy that coincides with children's developmental level. For instance, teachers might withhold certain activities from students as punishment. Unfortunately, this limitation of autonomy will often have the opposite effect than expected. When a child has been prevented from learning the very activities that promise independence, he may try even harder to do exactly what the teacher is restricting.

When schools restrict a student's autonomy, they restrict his drive to pursue need satisfaction. Consider what happens if an adult goes too far in restricting a child's food. When an adult deprives a child of food, the child may develop an extreme resentment towards the adult. He will also spend most of his waking moments plotting strategies for getting more food. When their autonomy is overly restricted, students become obsessed with the pursuit of independence. They will find other ways to assert their autonomy; therefore, teachers must have effective methods of helping students grow into responsible and independent citizens without unduly restricting their sense of self-determination.

Often, teachers resent having to deal with behavioral issues instead of teaching academics. However, once a person chooses a career in teaching children, she has no choice. The need for autonomy cannot be shut off any more than the need for food can be eliminated. To be successful, teachers must become expert in helping students responsibly meet their needs. We will further address this issue in subsequent chapters; however, an example here might help clarify the point. Suppose a child is getting in trouble on the playground. Many educators would recommend that the child be forbidden to use the playground until he can do so without getting in trouble. However, restricting his freedom does not solve the problem. Unless he has access to the playground, he can never learn to be responsible there. Because the child does not have the self-discipline to manage his own behavior in that setting, teachers often forbid him the opportunity to learn. The moment a student is restricted from playing, moving, and being autonomous, he may become obsessed with those issues. The student may be rendered nearly incapable of learning until other solutions are found. While teachers cannot allow a student to endanger himself or others, neither can they restrict his ability to learn. Teachers must have methods to solve the problem while helping the child develop responsible behavior in various situations. Our methods were devised to do both.

Teachers may understand how the need of autonomy makes teaching harder; however, they seldom understand how they can benefit from this need. Autonomy is essential for normal development. As teachers learn the methods we describe, they will come to understand that the need for autonomy provides great benefits for teachers. When students can responsibly manage their autonomy, teachers will see an improvement in self-confidence, better relationships with other students and adults, and a natural motivation to learn. Students can then focus on learning. The very definition of the word autonomy — freedom of will — makes the point; people have a built-in need to be self-sufficient. With the right methods, teachers can use the need for autonomy to develop students who are motivated to discipline their own behavior and become educated. Students will excel academically, because they are free to learn.

The need for socialization also has advantages and disadvantages for teachers. Students, like all humans, want friends and may be more concerned about making friends than about academic lessons. Despite this disadvantage, students' need for socialization is extremely important to teachers. This need has three separate advantages to teachers:

1. Students need friends or emotional connections with other people.
2. They need to belong or to be a part of an association of people.
3. They need social approval for their efforts.

These three parts to socialization are what makes classroom teaching possible. If teachers do not take advantage of these qualities of students, teaching becomes very difficult.

Educators often fail to appreciate that students need positive emotional connections with other children and with adults. This is a major advantage for teachers — students want the admiration of adults. In a classroom, the teacher may be the only adult; therefore, the teacher has the power to shape students into productive citizens who have a desire to achieve. However, this power comes with a risk. If the teacher abuses it, or does not facilitate positive emotional connections, she loses much of her influence, and much of the power is transferred to peers. Under these circumstances many students will come to care more about what their friends think than about the teacher. Students need to make friends in a way that promotes responsible citizenship in school and society, but they cannot depend on peers for guidance regarding right and wrong. In later chapters, we will describe how teachers can use the need for emotional connections to help students master their academic material and behave appropriately.

The need for friends is closely tied to the need to belong and can be satisfied without going to school. Gangs, for instance, create a sense of belonging. If schools are to compete with gangs, teachers must create a sense of affiliation for students to their class and school. Students must trust that the teacher cares about their best interests. However, this aspect of the need for socialization is what gives schools an incredible advantage in serving students. Classrooms are ready made for creating a sense of belonging. When students feel a strong sense of belonging to a class, they will show a greater ability to function within the expectations for classrooms. If schools use the advantage of the need to belong, schools will succeed and gangs will have difficulty surviving.

The third aspect of socialization, the need for social approval, is a powerful reinforcer and therefore valuable in creating success in the classroom. Teachers, by the nature of their position, have extensive control over social approval, and as a result the ability to get students to behave appropriately and to work for academic accomplishments. Despite the conveniences or inconveniences of human needs, such is the nature of the species teachers chose to teach. To be effective, they have no choice except to become proficient in methods dictated by the nature of students.

For teachers to get students to behave and work they must understand how to influence student behavior. However, many of the behavior management programs we see used in schools are inconsistent with the science of human behavior. We expect many teachers, when reading that previous sentence to be struck in disbelief. Teachers might think, "That cannot possibly be true. No one would expect us to use methods that are inconsistent with the science of human behavior." Nevertheless, the statement is true. Teachers' preparation seldom prepares them to understand the complexities of behavioral psychology, neuropsychology, and group dynamics. Teachers accept the methods in good faith and wonder in frustration why many students do not respond as expected. Too often, behavior management programs used in schools promote methods based on an incomplete or inaccurate understanding of human behavior. By the 1960s the behavioral research necessary to understand student behavior had been completed. However, the neurological research for understanding the brain and emotions comes from studies in the last 10 to 20 years.

Years ago the research on human behavior held considerable promise for educators. However, behavior analysts' advice to teachers on applying their ideas to schools was often not feasible. It was often more fitting for a research setting than a school. Those advisors were frustrated because schools could not be molded into research settings and educators were equally frustrated because if the science were to be of any use to them, it had to fit within their budgets and time constraints. The time constraints on teachers made it impossible for them to collect the data researchers considered essential. Unfortunately, educators, without a sufficient background in the underlying science, were left to design classroom applications on their own. The result is that many behavioral management concepts used in schools are not consistent with the science.

More than 70 years ago research into the behavior of mammals and birds found that when a reinforcing stimulus followed a behavior, the behavior increased in frequency. Those findings were confirmed with studies of human behavior. Subsequent research with animals also suggested that when a punishing stimulus followed a behavior, the behavior decreased in frequency. For obvious reasons, little experimentation has been done on the effects of punishment on student behavior. Nevertheless, teachers concluded punishment would reduce unwanted behavior with students. The leap seemed reasonable because parents had used punishment with children for centuries. In schools, behavior management systems introduced the theory that threats, warnings, and consequences would be an effective and less contentious way to reduce inappropriate behavior. However, schools never conducted long-term empirical research regarding the questions of effectiveness, side effects, or alternative methods. An understanding of classical conditioning and the basic science of human behavior would suggest inevitable and undesirable effects associated with warnings, threats, and negative consequences. We know of no instances where schools have conducted objective observations of how students respond to threats and warnings. However, our experience has confirmed those concerns and raised additional concerns about the broader scope of how threats and consequences affect other members in group settings.

Educators ignored other important findings of basic behavioral research. Animal studies designed to increase the frequency of behaviors used primary reinforcers that were naturally reinforcing for animals. Food was the only one that could be manipulated for experimentation. In working with animals, it served as the perfect reinforcer. To this day, those involved in training animals use food as the universal reinforcer. To enhance food's reinforcing power, experimenters routinely withheld it from animals; therefore, the subjects only had access to food during experimental conditions. Withholding food at other times prevented a satiation effect during experimentation.

The implications of these findings for education would infer the need for using primary reinforcers and preventing satiation effects. Social approval is the only primary reinforcer teachers can manipulate in a classroom. Fortunately, social approval is a natural reinforcer and students do not satiate on teacher approval. However, many behavioral management studies suggested extensive use of secondary reinforcers such as activities, privileges, and small toys. This adaptation made it difficult to immediately follow important behaviors with a reinforcer. As a result, educators frequently used tokens or points that students could later exchange for the secondary reinforcers (toys or activities). This process introduced a conditioned reinforcer (tokens or points) into the equation and further diluted the motivational power of secondary reinforcers.

Many teachers found the token system difficult to use in classrooms, and they correctly concluded that the results seldom justified the trouble. Attempting to simplify the process, teachers have frequently used secondary reinforcers based on an assessment of behavior over a period of time — perhaps 30 minutes. Unfortunately, the change violated the most absolute condition of behavioral science. A reinforcer can only strengthen a behavior if it immediately follows the behavior. Delaying the reinforcer for several minutes will result in no reinforcing value with animals and at best a very weak influence on human behavior. Some professionals will try to make delayed reinforcers more effective by describing to students why they earned the reinforcer. A description would be the only way to cognitively bridge the time gap between the specific behavior and the reinforcer, although that process is much less effective than teachers may assume. Even with older students, an effort to bridge the gap created by delayed reinforcers is minimally effective. Despite it having only a small fraction of the power needed to manage classroom behavior, many teachers still use delayed reinforcement systems as part of behavior management programs. But because the temporal relationship between the behavior and the reinforcer is paramount, teachers should realize that delaying a reinforcer will result in losing most or even all of the reinforcing effect.

Sometimes we get arguments from teachers that students respond very well to their expressions of appreciation. Although students want to hear such comments from their teacher, nearly all power to change the student's behavior is lost. We view all delayed descriptions as similar to a summation used in academic work. When a student writes a good paragraph, teachers will summarize their remarks by saying the paragraph was well written. However, to write a good paragraph the student must have previously learned to punctuate, capitalize, and write complete, grammatically correct sentences. Also, he had to learn to compose complete ideas consisting of several points. The summary assessment by a teacher expresses her appreciation for the efforts and will encourage the student to use what he has learned in the future. However, such a summation cannot help a student develop the skills necessary to write a paragraph.

The same would be true for a student who could behave very well for the entire morning. A summary evaluation would let a student know that the teacher noticed and appreciated his behavior. Nevertheless, that evaluation would do nothing to teach students specifically how to behave in class. For a particular student who behaves well in class, an occasional evaluative comment is fine. Unfortunately, many delayed assessments are used with students who need to learn specific behaviors. Most students will be delighted their teacher recognized their efforts for the last 30 minutes. However, students appreciating the kindness does not mean the specific and necessary behaviors were strengthened. In fact, those students who can behave appropriately for 30 minutes do not require much reinforcement to maintain their behavior. Teachers must have a process for strengthening the appropriate behaviors of otherwise disruptive students. Any effective methodology must be directed at strengthening particular behaviors with particular students.

Earlier in this chapter, we discussed how the need for social approval is a primary reinforcer. Social approval is the universal reinforcer for students. It is of great benefit to teachers that students will not satiate on social approval. For all practical purposes, psychological needs are not subject to satiation. Social approval will be effective all day every day. For example, a simple statement from a teacher describing how hard a student is working has more motivational power than any other technique available.

Another factor of animal research has frequently been overlooked. All animal studies were conducted with animals in captivity, the only way to assure they would not flee the experimental apparatus. Many students in Animal Behavior 101 learned this lesson the hard way. Readers can imagine the chaos as a careless student chased a rat through university classrooms. Captivity served several important roles in animal research that have different implications for creating programs in classrooms. As mentioned above, because subjects were captive, researchers could withhold food except during periods of experimentation. Captivity also assured that no extraneous lessons were learned during the period necessary for experiments to be completed. Teachers cannot control these factors in classrooms.

Behavioral research with animals, studied the use of punitive stimuli. They found that when a behavior was followed by a punitive stimulus, the behavior decreased in frequency. Because all teachers will face difficult student behavior, the use of punitive stimuli also made its way into educational methods. However, even from the data available 50 years ago, a more careful consideration of the application to schools would have been well advised. Because students are not caged like animals, they are technically non-captive subjects. They go home at the end of the school day. However, because of compulsory education laws we must consider how aversive stimuli affect students as both captive and non-captive subjects. Consider an animal researcher who dared to use punitive stimuli with non-captive subjects; he would have spent the remainder of his day trying to catch the subject. The subject, whether it was a rat, pigeon, or other primate would have flown the coop, so to speak.

Most educators assume the human brain is programed to inhibit certain behaviors in the presence of aversive stimuli. However, that is not so; instead, the innate response is to avoid the situation. For example, a young boy set out to train his dog and reprimanded the dog every time the dog failed to follow a command. His dog simply ran away; the natural response for the dog was to avoid the boy. Through a classical conditioning process, the boy became an undesirable companion. The boy could not train a dog that was miles away. Because elementary students are compelled to attend school, we must examine how the human brain responds when constantly on guard to the potential of aversive stimuli.

In the presence of aversive stimuli, the hippocampus and the amygdala remain on high alert for any further distress. Because distress is painful to adults and even more to children, the brain assigns the greatest importance to preventing or minimizing the psychological pain and not to learning the academic material. As a result, when the potential for distress is present, students have a difficult time concentrating on lessons. Nevertheless, with many current teaching methods, the potential for distress remains ever present. When teachers use aversive stimuli, they are assuming students can process the information and reach a conclusion that certain behaviors are unacceptable. However, understanding that behavior is unacceptable is a cognitive issue; it is nearly impossible following aversive stimuli. Students who are apprehensive of potential stress will find it difficult to ignore signals from the emotional center of the brain (amygdala), and process academic information through the prefrontal cortex. Because of these issues, many methods commonly used in classrooms are contraindicated. When students are anticipating a classmate will soon be in trouble, learning becomes difficult for the best students and nearly impossible for others.

In schools, students are essentially captive at least until the age of sixteen. Even if a student were to run out of the school building, he would be found and returned to class. Though students, for all practical purposes, are captive, educators cannot assume that student behavior can be eliminated much like animal behavior. Furthermore, another effect noted in animal research has significant implications for educators. Subjecting captive animals to punishment resulted in undesirable side effects. These side effects were most obvious with the random application of punitive stimuli. In experimental applications, where one experimenter is working with one subject, nearly perfect consistency is possible. However, perfect consistency is never possible in classrooms where one teacher is teaching 25 students. Readers might get a chuckle out of imagining an animal experimenter attempting to conduct 25 experiments simultaneously. Now imagine that experiment with all of the rats in the same cage. Irregular application of punishment in classrooms approximates random application in experimental conditions, and the effect of random application of aversive stimuli with primates closely resembles insanity in humans. The fact that students in schools experience psychological pain instead of physical pain does not negate the effects. In classrooms, teachers cannot avoid the negative effects of punishment. When we explain this to teachers, some say it is like kicking them in the stomach. They do not respond this way because they want to punish students, but because they know the difficulty of behavioral problems in schools. They feel, following this explanation, that teaching just became impossible. However, we will describe effective procedures that eliminate the need to use most negative consequences while making teaching easier. Our methodology will consider the value of behavioral research and account for the realities of teaching heterogeneous groups in crowded classrooms.

Besides the inconsistency issues, different effects and side effects will be observed with students than with laboratory animals. Rats and pigeons have few alternative responses except to run or fly away. Although we suspect that if experimenters had chosen lions as their subjects, some punishment experiments would have ended with the lion being perfectly contented after having devoured the experimenter. Children have more ways to establish their autonomy than animals. If the possibility existed, we expect many students experiencing coercive methods would leave school and not go back. For elementary students, however, two reasons make this alternative infeasible. Besides the compulsory education laws, elementary students understand they are dependent on adults for their safety and survival needs. Because of the intelligent nature of humans, younger students will usually refrain from running away, but nevertheless prove they are autonomous. Coercion may prompt or perhaps even impel a coerced student into inappropriate behavior. Students can, and some will, become rebellious, defiant, or unreachable in their resistance to coercion.

In the last 20 years, research into neuroscience has provided a basic understanding about how some aspects of the human brain works. The hippocampus and the amygdala stand alert to detect any threat to the individual. Upon detection of a threat, the amygdala commands action before sending the information to the prefrontal cortex, the reasoning center of the brain. The amygdala, without consultation, directs either a fight, flight, or freeze response to save the individual's life. Anyone who has happened upon a rattlesnake or had a baseball rapidly approaching his head, can be thankful that the amygdala dictates an immediate response. Had the information been sent to the prefrontal cortex for analysis and computation of the most reasonable response, the available time for a lifesaving response may have elapsed. Fortunately, students rarely encounter these conditions in classrooms. However, stress and anxiety are also first processed by the amygdala, which may never send the information to the prefrontal cortex for processing. However, if the information can get through to the prefrontal cortex, the response may be highly influenced by the child's previous experiences. Those students, who have experienced the greatest anxiety in their lives will be least able to handle the situation.

When stress or anxiety is present for long periods, chronic significant problems develop. Under conditions of chronic stress the prefrontal cortex becomes incapable of inhibiting a fear response from the amygdala and a rational response is impossible. The amygdala, functioning without the ability to reason, takes charge of the response and teachers should expect many irrational responses. Students may respond with fear or aggression. In schools, aggressive responses often result in more consequences and more stress for all students. This can lead to chronic pathological behaviors and even permanent pathological changes to the brain. Whereas the prefrontal cortex has enough plasticity eventually to recover from chronic stress, the same is not true for the amygdala and the hippocampus.

Some teachers will argue that permanent pathological changes may explain the difficulty they are having with some students. But because permanent damage may have resulted from experiences in schools or other settings does not mean those students cannot function in school. Schools can still work with those students. Neurological findings suggest that by keeping anxiety to a minimum, schools can provide an appropriate learning environment for all students. A child with permanent pathological changes to the brain could then still function appropriately in school and other environments. The findings suggest that they do not function very well in highly stressful situations. Classrooms do not have to be stressful to students. For instance, a student Art served for three years did very well in his program, but did not do well in a public school program that used lots of negative consequences. When he was moved to a different public school program, he was assigned to a teacher who never raised her voice and created lots of success. He did fine in that school for three years. In his fourth year, he was again assigned to a much more negative teacher and did not do well.

Emotions also play an important role in memory. Studies have shown that long-term memory is dependent on emotion. Unless an emotion attends information, the memory will be lost in just a few minutes. Also, for information to be readily available in practical situations, the memory must be attended by positive emotions. The chronic stress and anxiety mentioned above inhibit both how information is remembered and its recall. These findings have broad implications for teaching. In order for schools to reach academic goals for nearly all students, teachers need methods for establishing and maintaining a positive emotional climate in their classrooms. Despite these findings being recent, the effects are not new. The same factors have affected learning throughout our history.

Having considered these issues, we will return to what must happen in schools. To learn in school, the student's prefrontal cortex must successfully inhibit the need to stay in motion without inhibiting the desire for intellectual stimulation. All creatures learn best when in constant motion, and rest their brains and bodies when not in motion. In schools, students are expected to learn while at rest. However, because learning under those conditions is possible and some students succeed, teachers are blindsided by how difficult it is for others. This issue is further confused by how easily students inhibit the need to move about when playing video games. However, video games require rapid fine motor movement, and provide instant and constant reinforcers for game accomplishments. All of this happens while the player limits gross motor movement. Students cannot produce a correct academic response every second. If they could, a teacher would be a bit overwhelmed to reinforce all such responses in a class of 25 students. However, teachers can use specific methods to accomplish similar results. Three neurological requirements must happen:

1. Powerful and random reinforcers would have to follow instances of (a) a student inhibiting movement, and (b) exhibiting behaviors that promote learning and academic accomplishments.
2. The prefrontal cortex would have to accept the importance of the assigned tasks.
3. The prefrontal cortex could not be overwhelmed with emotional issues sent from the amygdala.

Without a process specifically designed to accomplish this threefold feat, nearly half of all students will struggle in school. A more precise description would be that half the prefrontal cortexes will struggle to focus on academic learning.

Question and Answer

At the end of most of the remaining chapters we have answered a question or two regarding the application of the issues discussed in the chapter. When we present, we always like to answer questions, and these are some of the best we have encountered.

Question: The research you cite seems to imply that all students with permanent brain pathology should be separated into special classrooms and not served in regular classrooms?

Answer: Currently, schools cannot reliably determine which students have permanent changes to the hippocampus or amygdala. Even so, the most cost-effective solution would be to significantly reduce the stress in all classrooms. Not only would that address the behavioral problems of certain students, but it would improve the academic progress of all students.

Question: I have a student who is adopted and he seems always to be in fight or flight mode, as you put it. How can I get him to trust me?

Answer: This is a perfect question. Chapter Five will help answer this question. However, remember this boy has spent several years of his life not trusting adults. Gaining his trust will be neither easy nor quick. For now we will limit our answer to just two points. First, be gentle with him. Second, calm his emotions and try to get him to cognitively process the issue. The more times he can process information with his prefrontal cortex, the closer you are getting him to recognize trust. However, in subsequent chapters you will learn to create a positive culture. Once you have a positive culture in place, that will do much of the work and children will change for the better with little direct effort from you.

Summary

- Teachers must understand how human needs affect learning.
- For students to learn in school, the prefrontal cortex must successfully inhibit the need to stay in constant motion. This cannot happen for

any given student if the amygdala becomes aroused and preempts the prefrontal cortex.

- For a response to be learned, a reinforcing stimulus must follow the behavior.

- Punitive stimuli, following a response, do not result in elimination of the response, but instead prompt the student to avoid the situation or become aggressive.

- Classical conditioning describes how some students come to fear or even hate school.

- Primary reinforcers, or reinforcers that satisfy a need, are the most powerful reinforcers.

- Reinforcers can only be effective when they immediately follow the targeted response. A delayed reinforcer may, at best, have a weak and unreliable effect in strengthening a response.

3

Teaching Is a Group Activity

ART WATCHED AS THE YOUNG TEACHER, Jana, worked with her kindergarten class of 17 students. Nine of them were typical students one could have found in any kindergarten classroom. However, eight were in this program because they had serious mental health problems, including reactive attachment disorder, oppositional defiant disorder, and bipolar disorder.

He watched as she taught sounds associated with letters. She taught the sounds made by the letters "p" and "t." She taught the sound associated with the letter "a." After all of the students had gotten each sound right several times, she handed out worksheets. The first worksheet was to practice writing several lowercase letters, but one student soon noticed the student next to him was writing uppercase letters. He criticized the other student and said, "Those are uppercase letters. You're dumb." Jana immediately stopped the students and asked who could explain the common purpose of their class. A girl raised her hand and said, "It is for everyone to learn as much as we can this year."

Jana smiled and replied, "That's exactly right." She continued, "Andy what's the purpose of this class?"

Andy answered, "It's for everyone to learn as much as they can."

Jana said, "Exactly. What do we all need to do if everyone is to succeed?"

Mari raised her hand. Jana called on her and asked, "Can you explain what we need to do?"

Mari answered, "We have to help each other do good."

Jana said, "That is terrific. I think you all know how to help everyone be successful. Does it help to criticize each other?"

Many students shouted in unison, "No, it hurts."

Jana shouted her answer, "All of you are right!" She continued, "It hurts our class. We're here to help each other. When we see someone making a mistake what can we do?" Two hands went up. Jana called on Conner.

Conner explained, "We could tell the person nicely what he was doing wrong."

Jana said, "That's right. Would you get in trouble for talking in class?"

Conner answered, "No, unless we talked too loud."

"Good, we could help each other. What else could we do?" Lili raised her hand.

"Lili."

Lili answered, "I could tell you that someone needed help."

Jana said, "That's right. You could get me to help them. We will all need help sometime. Good job. Let's get back to work."

Teaching is inherently a group activity and that makes all the difference. Humans (students in this case) respond differently in groups than in individual situations. Some important variables of working with groups are non-factors when working with individuals.

First Fundamental: A Common Purpose

For a group to be functional, members must unify to accomplish a common purpose. When a class of students unifies as a group, all students can excel. Each student must work for the good of the group and for his own success. When a common cause is in place, every student shares in the success of the group and the success of each student encourages every other student.

Students can and must have individual goals; nevertheless, members can unite for a common purpose. A group can become either functional or dysfunctional, but unless the group is functional, not all students will succeed. Unification for a common cause is one essential part of a functional group. In a dysfunctional class, many students will fail to meet their individual goals, and the class will fail to meet its collective goals.

The collective goal of any class should be for virtually every student to achieve well above grade level criteria.

Similarities exist between classes, teams, and other groups. Good coaches understand that teams must unite for a common purpose because without a united team, success will be elusive. Individuals may have to sacrifice their own goals for the sake of the team. For example, a basketball player who hopes to play guard may have to play forward for the sake of the team. Fortunately, in classrooms students never have to sacrifice their goals for the sake of the class. Every student can excel without impeding the progress of others. However, sometimes students must temporarily put the class ahead of their own work.

In classrooms, students can impede the success of others by being disruptive or by criticizing other students. In the example above, Jana responded when a student criticized another student and all students were reminded that she did not approve of students criticizing each other. However, she did not criticize the offending student, because, if she had, that student and others would be fearful of being shamed in the future. Also, students who disrupt the class impede the success of other students. Having a tantrum, making noises, or distracting other students affects the progress of everyone. Many teachers will realize that getting all students to eliminate disruptive behavior is difficult. In this book, we describe the necessary skills to manage any group of students to work together for the benefit of everyone. These skills are much easier to master than most teachers may think.

Successful teaching frequently involves encouraging students to volunteer some of their time to help others excel. Usually, helping others means students will become more successful, but another benefit also becomes apparent. Students who are committed to the success of the class will be less likely to disrupt others. With a unified purpose comes greater cooperation and students who have helped others will be delighted when others succeed. We urge teachers to recognize that students who help others are not sacrificing their own accomplishments; they will learn more and score higher on end-of-year exams because of being part of a unified group.

Several students in Mark Draper's sixth grade class were having difficulty with long division. He had gone over the material several times and had several students come to the board to work problems. Finally he had the students start on worksheets. In just a few minutes, a half-dozen students had their hands in the air signaling they needed help. It would take a long time for him to help all of them. He asked two of the better students in the class if they would stop their work and volunteer to help other students. Both students were delighted to help others, and in just a few minutes, all students were working independently.

While the exact wording they use may vary from teacher to teacher, the common purpose is for every student to reach his potential both personally and academically. Teachers must be successful in getting students to work together in pursuit of that purpose. Students being unified for a common cause means that while each student is pursuing his own goals, he never interferes with other students pursuing theirs. All students should take pride in the class being successful. They should be as concerned about the success of the group as they are their own achievement. The unified purpose will benefit every student in pursuit of their accomplishments and the methods described in later chapters will help students understand that every student is an important part of the class.

Many teams and groups are assembled to compete with others. In competition, for every winner there is a corresponding loser; fortunately, in classrooms and schools, this type of competition is not necessary. One student can do superior work without any detrimental effect on other students — no one loses. The fact that some students will do better than others is inevitable, but does not present a problem. However, when classrooms, or groups within classrooms, compete, problems may become evident. Some educators hope to take advantage of the competitive spirit to get maximum effort from students. However, in academic work, having a few students who lose is not advantageous, because those who lose will find ways to pull others down with them.

Students need to learn to persevere even through difficult material. Teachers want students to continue working even after doing poorly on some work. When teachers understand how to build cooperation and simultaneously develop perseverance, competition will seem unnecessary.

Teachers want each student to be proud of individual success, but students should also be proud of their class. Teachers can help students understand that it is not about being better than others. Instead, education is about every student learning to strive and excel. The group concept of a classroom is a little like a choir — they must sing together to be the best they can be. Some members will have better voices than others, but the objective is for the choir to be the best possible. Education should not be an endeavor designed to see who will fail; teachers should design classrooms to help everyone succeed.

In our culture, escaping the desire to be better than everyone else is difficult. Parents want to know how their child compares with others and students want to be better than other students. If teachers give in to these demands, they help create a culture of success and failure in which many students will fail. For all students to reach their potential, teachers must create a culture of universal proficiency. The goal, in every classroom, is for each student to do his best. The question facing teachers is how to get students to be concerned about their own success, and be happy for other students who are doing well.

With our training, many teachers have been successful in many settings. We are confident that most teachers, upon finishing this book, will understand how to get nearly every student to reach grade level criteria in reading, writing, math, and science. Students will soon excel. Teachers will ask about two important issues. First, they want to know how much of their time the use of these methods will consume. The answer is a little more at the beginning of the year and much less after the first few weeks. Second, they want to know how long it will take students to show remarkable progress. When the methods are applied correctly throughout a school year students will make excellent progress before the end of the school year. However, teachers will usually see considerable improvement from most students in two or three months. However, we have learned to expect considerable variation between students. One of the more surprising variations is that some students will make little progress for the first seven months and still be ready for the next grade before the end. By adopting these techniques teachers will have more time, not less, to dedicate to academic work, and the school experience will become more positive for students and teachers.

For students to reach the ultimate level of achievement they must work together and accept responsibility for everyone's success. That is the nature of a successful group. Every student accomplishes more because everyone succeeds. The objective is to get every student to have a positive influence on the success of the group and the group to have a positive influence on every student. We call this a *positive culture*. This issue of a positive culture is a recurring concept throughout this book. When teachers effectively create a positive culture, every student in class will succeed.

Second Fundamental: Teachers as Leaders

By helping a group develop a common purpose, an effective leader takes an important step towards building a functional group. Unfortunately, teachers get very little leadership training, but must be effective leaders. Frequently, they must develop these skills on the job. The result has been that many teachers have only a few of the leadership skills required to get students to work together as a functional group.

An essential characteristic of good leaders is that they have clear expectations of how they want those they lead to behave. Teachers must clearly define expectations for themselves and their students. The functionality of the class will suffer unless all expectations for every situation are made clear. A strong leader has a vision of her goals and makes them happen, thus developing a program that is successful for all students. An effective leader of young children creates confidence that every student will succeed. Confidence always begins with the teacher; the most effective teachers we know have complete confidence in their skills to make every child successful. However, these teachers would say that their confidence was enhanced by learning the skills of interactive teaching.

One of the worst things a leader can do is to make excuses for group members who fail. That is also true for teachers. Effective teachers do not make excuses for failing students; they find ways to help them excel. Teachers must accept that they are accountable for student success and know that through their leadership every student will succeed. A good leader never gives a student an excuse for failure because the students would have it on good authority that they cannot succeed. Teachers will find it to be equally damaging to accept excuses from students or parents. Teachers must remember that all failure is only temporary, until a solution can be found. They must avoid excuses and concentrate on solutions instead of problems. Leaders need to understand that no matter what is happening in a child's life, he can succeed. For example, a child who had been beaten into a coma by adoptive parents overcame his constant fear of adults to succeed in school. The child's recovery was possible because teachers used their interactions to promote healing.

Teachers also must be careful never to make excuses for their own shortcomings. When a teacher uses excuses, she has essentially taught students that failure can be explained away. We remember an example of a teacher who was assigned to serve 24 students in a classroom built for 12 special education students. She could have made an excuse claiming that accomplishing her goals in that classroom was impossible, but she did not. Despite the disadvantages, by the end of the year her students achieved superior academic results.

For a classroom to function properly, the teacher and students must maintain emotional regulation — the ability to modulate emotions through many situations and over considerable periods of time. As a leader, teachers must be certain they set the standard and model emotional control. They will face many challenging situations. Even if a student destroys a classroom, or hurts another student, the teacher must be a model for appropriate behavior. By this we mean she will maintain her composure and deal with the behavior in a rational manner. A teacher who loses control has taught her students that having a tantrum is okay. If teachers do not want their students to overreact, they must be sure they do not. Teachers who want students to express their emotions with words must model such behavior for their students. Teachers who want their students to work even harder when something goes wrong must show how to do just that.

Unfortunately, teachers will encounter situations where a student will interfere with how the class functions. In other organizations, a member who violates rules may be dismissed from the group. Because elementary education is mandatory, educators have limited options. Teachers must have reliable methods for helping students develop responsible behavior. We will describe those methods, which are possible and attainable.

With many groups, a choir for example, members joined to pursue a common purpose. However, elementary classrooms include members who are not excited about the central purpose. Because students are not voluntary members, of either the school or the classroom, a methodology to develop unity is essential. Also, consider that the pursuit of academic accomplishments is not intrinsically reinforcing to students. Upon enrollment in kindergarten or first grade only a few students will immediately understand the importance of education. Many students will find the work laborious and confusing. These factors combine to create the perfect recipe for disaster. Too often teachers do not have the necessary methods to create success. Nevertheless, administrators may pressure them to achieve remarkable results despite not having the necessary skills. Teachers need procedures to get young students to voluntarily and energetically pursue learning. When all factors are considered, it is nothing short of amazing that the problems in elementary classrooms are not worse. To be effective leaders, teachers must have a clear understanding of the methodology necessary to help students achieve. Teachers need to have confidence in the process.

Strong leadership implies positive leadership. Nothing is ever gained by being unpleasant. The first goal for a teacher is to get students to trust she will help them succeed. They must trust that she will help them get along with others and not let them be bullied. Students must trust their teacher never to shame them in front of their peers. The teacher who stands up for every child has demonstrated that students can count on her to be an advocate for everyone. Of everything a teacher will do, developing and maintaining trust is the most elemental.

Students need to understand that some classroom rules are necessary; however, they should never be afraid of violating a rule. Because they are students, they will make mistakes. Sometimes they will forget, because forgetting is an inescapable part of learning. The teacher is not there to punish mistakes, but to create success. An important goal of education, is for students to make fewer mistakes with each passing day. However, if students are afraid of making mistakes, they will make more of them.

Consistent with principles of leadership, effective teachers will develop rationales for students needing to learn the academic material. For instance, Cari explains to her classes that we must learn our letters so we can learn to read. She might say, "We are practicing our sight words so we can be level-four readers." She repeatedly describes what they are learning and why. She frequently uses big vocabulary such as, "We are going to math centers so we can learn to compose and decompose our numbers to ten." The ideal would be that every student, at the end of the day, could describe what they had learned that day and the reason it was important. To excel, students must understand the importance of learning.

One aspect of leadership is to create success. Cari assures the success of every student every day. While every student is not going to do equally well, every student in her class is successful every day. Some students may require simplified lessons or more help; nevertheless, they must still be successful. When students routinely get recognition for their success every day, it generates the essential attribute of self-confidence all students need to reach their potential. Students cannot excel unless they persistently strive to do their best and they will strive when they have developed the confidence to succeed. A major objective of teachers is to never undermine the confidence of any student.

Many methods are discussed in later chapters, but we will insert a description of one at this point to help readers envision how these goals can be accomplished. As part of recognition for accomplishments, Cari might have all students celebrate something a particular student had accomplished. The purpose is for the celebration to serve as a reinforcer for the work that led to the accomplishment. However, by having all students recognize the accomplishment she has also helped the students understand the class is unified for the benefit of all students. For instance, she had the class celebrate that Jaime had passed level one for sight words. A moment later they were as happy, but not any more happy, that Julie had passed level 18. No one was ever allowed to make Jaime feel inferior or Julie feel superior.

If Julie were to say, "Ha, ha, I'm at level 18." Cari would immediately say, "Jamie needs to be proud of how she is doing. I know I am proud of her and you never know, we might be needing her help in a few days. If this work is hard for some of you, we will just keep at it until it is easy." The reader will notice she did not let it go. Neither did she use a consequence for Julie's words. She did not want to hurt Julie's feelings any more than she would accept Jamie's feelings being hurt. She made it clear that she did not approve of students criticizing each other. However, the task is to help Julie, not to shame her. Cari will remember to approach Julie the next time they celebrate her success. She will walk over to Julie, bend down and whisper in her ear, "We are going to celebrate how well you are doing, please do not hurt the feelings of others." Readers will recognize this as another example of never inflicting damage to the confidence or trust of any student.

Schools have never placed much emphasis on developing a class into a group with a unified purpose. Perhaps out of necessity, coaches of sports teams have developed more skills for using the team to help each member excel. At this juncture, we want to make a point: teaching a group is different from teaching one individual. Group dynamics, however, can be an advantage, not a disadvantage, to teachers.

Classrooms are very complex environments, as we will examine in the next several chapters. However, because teams are a little less complex, an example from a sports team will better illustrate the two fundamentals we have described. This example describes a cheerleading team. The team was made up of eleven girls, ages nine and ten, and coached by Jana, the teacher from earlier in this chapter, when she was just seventeen. This team competed in the Sierra Youth Football League, which is a national organization for football and cheerleading. While the league is not as well-known as Pop Warner, it is respected in the western United States. Several observers who saw an early practice considered this team the clumsiest group of girls they had ever seen. When a man asked the coach, "What can you do with such clumsy girls?" the young coach answered, "They will become the best they can be. What more would you ask?" The authors think that statement would be a worthy axiom for all educators.

Our intention is not to describe everything about coaching cheerleaders. Instead we will describe the coach's leadership and how she got the girls to work as a team. At one early practice, several girls complained about not being able to do the routines she was teaching. She said, "Girls stop. We have a new rule. You are not allowed to use the word, 'can't.' You can say something is hard, or you can tell me that you need more practice. You can ask for help, but you are not allowed to use the word 'can't.' That word is not in your vocabulary, and that word is not in my vocabulary." She never allowed herself even to think the girls could not learn to do the routine she developed. She taught, the girls practiced, and they improved a little bit every day. This young coach had just shown that she could lead a team, and would not let them erode their own confidence.

Once, several girls criticized another girl. They said, "Susan is holding us back. We would be better if she were any good."

Addressing the team, the coach said, "If she is holding you back, your job is to pull her up. There are ten of you and just one of her. You can lift her more than she can pull you down. The team's job is to help everyone do their best. Criticism will not help you and will not help her. When everyone is the best possible teammate you can be, no one can ask any more of you." This was a clear example of how the young coach molded the group into a team with a common purpose. She did not allow them to make excuses. Teachers can do the same in every classroom. Jana, as a leader, was working to never let one member hold the group back for long, and to help everyone succeed.

In the first competition, the team did not do very well. The cheerleaders were discouraged by the judges' comments. This coach insisted the girls not allow themselves to be discouraged. She insisted that the only issue was for them to keep improving. She said to the team, "The season is not over. We will continue getting better. Do not let these scores discourage you, just keep working. When the season is over, we will evaluate ourselves on whether we did our best. When you have done your best that is all you can do."

This coach could be considered an exemplary teacher, and later proved herself to be just that. Instead of teaching multiplication, she was teaching the girls a cheerleading routine. Her job was to be a leader and to help the girls excel to the limits of their ability. For them to be the best they could be, she had to get each of them to excel individually and to help every member of the team to do the same. Together they could accomplish more than any one girl could achieve.

At the end of the year they competed in the national SYFL tournament in Las Vegas. On the day of the competition they realized that the sponsor of the team had made a mistake. One girl had already turned 11. They would not be allowed to compete with the nine- and ten-year-old girls. Instead they would have to compete in the 11- and 12-year-old division. Many parents were upset. Some were upset with the sponsor and others were upset with the strictness of the rule. The parents were upsetting the girls so the young coach took charge, as a good leader should. She said, "Nothing has changed. At the beginning of the season, we said that our goal was to do the best we can do. The division we compete in does not prevent us from such a performance. We simply need to go out and do our routine to the best of our ability. If we do, this team will have earned my admiration, and your parents will be proud. I hope the judges can see how well you are doing, but we don't have control of what the judges think. We can only control what we do." Again, she had shown her leadership and got the girls to focus on their goal.

Typically, at cheerleading competitions teams practice throughout the day in hallways, parking lots, or any other place they can find to practice. This team did not do that. The coach told the team they were not going to practice. She explained, "We cannot get any better today. We need to make this a fun day and this afternoon we will have the privilege to show how well we can do our routine. We'll spend the day together, but you get to decide what we will do. We must conduct ourselves appropriately, but we will have a fun day." Over the season the team had become unified, and every girl supported every other cheerleader. This day of fun activities further solidified the team. With an effort to maintain their unity, the coach kept the team relaxed leading up to their performance. The fact the girls were clumsy at the beginning of the season was a non-factor by December. In their first competition, they got low scores from the judges, but did not let that discourage them. Earlier in the day they found out they would be competing in a higher division; nevertheless, this coach would not let the girls become discouraged or make excuses. On this day in December, these girls, unified by a strong leader, came together and performed to the best of their ability. Competing against 12 other teams, they won the SYFL national cheerleading championship for their division.

This is not a story about cheerleading. This story is about what every teacher can accomplish with every class in any school. Incidentally, the coach was using many methods described in this book and such results could not be attained with the methodology currently available to most teachers.

Three more fundamentals specific to groups will be briefly described in this chapter. Many particulars regarding these fundamentals will need to wait until the methods are described.

Third Fundamental: Anything That Affects One Student, Affects Everyone

A third fundamental of groups is that anything that affects one student affects all students.

This fundamental does not say every student will be affected the same. The meaning is straightforward: whatever has an impact on one student has an impact on every student. Every teacher interaction affects every student and every student's action or reaction affects all other students. Teachers must take into account the influence of their procedures on every member of the class. Teachers should understand that students will be less affected as they get older, but the fundamental also applies to adults. The most effective teachers are alert to how all students are reacting to events in their classroom.

How students are affected by everything that happens in a classroom has already been described in a couple of examples. For instance, in previous examples both Cari and Jana intervened to stop a student criticizing another student. If either teacher had only been concerned with the behavior of the offending student, they would not need to interrupt the entire class. However, criticism from one child had affected another child and therefore affected every student. Also, a teacher's actions will also affect all students. The offending student was not in a vacuum. The student perfectly understood the concept of affecting other students.

In each case, a student was trying to make himself superior in the eyes of the other students. How is it that teachers often miss a point readily understood by students?

Teachers using our methods avoid any direct reference to the offending student. By shaming the offending student a teacher would have an undesirable influence on all students. Every student would not be effected the same way. However, many students would lose trust in the teacher, because she might shame them as well.

The most important aspect of this fundamental is that it helps teachers create widespread success. The success of each student has a positive effect on every student. The improved self-confidence of one student influences every student. With each positive interaction, the teacher has a positive influence on every student. When students become unified for a common purpose, the impact will be beneficial to everyone. Leaders of groups, especially leaders of young children, must understand how to use every event, positive or negative, to promote universal success.

Fourth Fundamental: Use an Interactive Process That Develops Cooperation

All teacher-directed interactions have a favorable or unfavorable influence on everything related to learning. By using carefully chosen interactions, teachers will not only help individual students, but will also develop appropriate group behavior. When we speak of interactions, we are referring to what a teacher says to individual students and the group as a whole. However, as we will describe later what is not said, also influences student behavior. Effective interactions depend on several factors: what is said or not said, when it is said, to which student it is said, and how the teacher says it. The necessity of building cooperation between students and the importance of the school curriculum are equal. To get students to excel academically, they must learn to cooperate with the teacher and each other. Teachers can develop a cooperative culture by carefully selecting their interactions, and therefore create environments where every student excels.

Unfortunately, the interactive methods, which are always available to teachers, are seldom taught and not intuitive. Conversely, if teachers find themselves constantly needing new techniques to stop inappropriate behavior, they cannot succeed. Creating successful classrooms is instead dependent on teachers adopting an interactive process that promotes appropriate behavior.

When we ask different teachers how they want students to act and learn, we get much the same answer. Teachers want several things from students:

1. Teachers want students calmly to pursue learning.
2. They want students to be compliant with teacher instructions.
3. All students should be confident in their ability to learn.
4. Students should accept each other.
5. They should be cooperative.
6. Students should understand the importance of learning.

These attributes are within the reach of every student. By carefully planning a proactive process, teachers can create the cooperative culture where the best attributes are developed. These interactions and resulting attributes are the elements that allow Laura, Cari, and Jana to accomplish so much. We understand that such a process seems impossible because some students are doing everything possible to derail the teacher's plans. However, keep reading and the methods and the importance of those methods will become apparent.

One attribute that benefits students is the self-confidence that allows them to undertake almost any developmentally appropriate task and succeed. Many teachers have wished their students had greater self-confidence. However, in typical classrooms only some students develop it. The goal of all teachers should be gradually to increase the confidence of every student in the first six weeks of a school year. However, most teachers will be at a disadvantage because they will begin learning the methods during the school year and may slowly acquire the skills over several months. Many times they are attempting to integrate the new methods with what they have done in the past and the power of the new methods are compromised. However, Art has had teachers start developing their skills mid-year and still see incredible results with their students before the school year ended. For some teachers the process will take longer, but they should never give up. One teacher Art trained spent two years resisting the process and making excuses before she became an outstanding teacher.

Teachers can accomplish almost anything they want with any group of students. The issue is not the area of the city where they teach. Neither the parents nor the students can prevent success. The most important variable is the methodology the teacher chooses to use. Teachers can envision what they want their class to achieve and use positive methods to accomplish their goals. We have seldom seen teachers set their goals too high. More often we see teachers set their goals too low and limit the progress of the students.

Fifth Fundamental: Events May Have Different Effects When They Occur in a Group of Peers

People, particularly children, react differently in a group of peers than when they are interacting one on one with an adult. For instance, when a boy at home tells his mother how dumb another student is, it has no adverse effects, because neither another student nor the class is effected. The conversation is just between a boy and his mother. In class, however, as described in the example with the kindergarten teacher, the comment will have a broad impact. In group situations such criticism will affect the student and many other students as well. Students may become hypercritical, afraid of making a mistake, or overreactive to criticism. Two other typical reactions are that students may exhibit much less ability to regulate their emotions and may want to show their friends they will not accept criticism.

A primary issue in effective teaching is to understand the dynamics of groups. Many techniques from traditional methods could have a detrimental influence on other students. The techniques we propose are designed to avoid detrimental effects and to promote positive results throughout a class. Teachers will have greater success when they are sensitive to how students will respond in a group of peers. In fact, teachers themselves are subject to responding differently in a group of peers. We have often seen teachers choose their methods of handling misbehavior by selecting teaching methods based on the approval of other teachers.

Often teachers do very well until they must deal with a difficult student. The issues involved in handling difficult behavior often determine the effectiveness of various teaching methods, but teachers need not fear difficult students. In fact, with appropriate methods, difficult students will provide teachers the opportunity to gain the confidence of every student. Following is an example that shows what can be accomplished even with rebellious students and provides an example of the six attributes described earlier.

In the middle of March, in a kindergarten classroom, a boy jumped from his chair and raced across the room. He grabbed things from a cubby and threw them on the floor. The teacher shouted, "Dusty, stop!"

Dusty turned and ran the other direction. He kicked a waste basket, overturned a chair, and knocked an electronic notebook off a table. The teacher caught him and safely held him until help could arrive. He was taken to the office, and his mother was called to come to the school. After reviewing his records, administrators at his school found his behavior had gotten progressively worse throughout the year. Also, the most recent evaluation revealed no academic progress since the beginning of the year. The administration decided to revoke his variance and send him back to his neighborhood school. Schools frequently use a revocation of a variance to get out of serving a difficult student. Dusty started in Laura Gilmore's class the next morning. In this chapter, we will not describe the methods she used with Dusty. The methods will take up the remainder of the book. Instead, we will describe their progress over the last eight weeks of the school year. Often in schools, teachers have given up on some students by midyear. Before diving into the methods, we want to make the point that with the methods you are about to learn, students can change dramatically within a few minutes and make remarkable progress in just a few weeks.

Dusty's behavior gradually improved over the next two weeks. Laura worked hard to get him to care about learning. Despite her efforts, he lacked so much self-confidence that he made little academic progress during those first two weeks. However, the other students continued to tell him that he could do his work. In just a few more days, he started working hard at his lessons. Laura was determined to have him ready for first grade. With her methods, he worked and made progress every day. Over the next few weeks, his behavior for Laura was near-perfect, but he still had difficulty following the instructions for other teachers and a substitute.

Dusty also grew in other ways. He painted an excellent picture of a shark. He wanted to take it home to his mother. Laura had planned to display all the students' pictures on the wall. Dusty protested. Instead of giving in to prevent a tantrum, she recognized this as an excellent opportunity to teach him to accept disappointment. She pointed out that every student had wonderful pictures and they all wanted their parents to see their work. She continued, "You will all get to take your pictures home at the end of the year." While Dusty was disappointed, he did not have a tantrum.

In just eight weeks, the time for end-of-the-year testing had arrived. Despite the overwhelming odds, he had become determined to meet criteria for first grade in reading. The other students encouraged him. He took the test without fear. When the scores came back, all the students were excited by their scores. More than 80 percent had met or exceeded criteria. In just a few moments, the other students realized Dusty was not celebrating. His score was considered "approaching criteria." The teacher reminded him of how far he had come in eight weeks. The rest of the class broke into a spontaneous celebration for him. During that eight-week period he progressed from having virtually no reading skills to almost reaching criteria for first grade. He missed the criteria by just one point. He scored about equally well in math, although he struggled more with writing. Given appropriate teaching methods, Dusty went from nearly hopeless at age five to anything-is-possible in eight weeks and was promoted to first grade. Much of his progress was due to the positive effect of the other students. Besides the techniques Laura had used, the positive culture had also helped him. This teacher had built a culture of support from all the students. The way Dusty would react in this group of peers was different from how he would react in any other group.

Question and Answer

Question: It seems impossible to me that students would care about how other students are doing.

Answer: The answer to this question will become more apparent throughout this book. When teachers succeed in creating unity within a class they will most likely be astonished at how students take pride in each other's success. We have seen students from preschool through the eighth grade genuinely care about the success of others. Both of the authors have worked at developing this phenomenon and seen the results for about 20 years. Students as young as three years of age can work together for the good of the group. We have seen students helping each other even in classes serving students who were seriously disturbed.

Summary

- Because teaching is a group activity, different teaching methods are necessary.
- For groups to be functional, a common purpose is necessary.
- More students will meet their individual goals when the students work for everyone's benefit.
- Groups are seldom successful unless they have a strong leader.
- In classes, anything that affects one student will affect every student.
- Leaders must use an interactive process that develops cooperation.
- Events do not have the same effect in groups as they would in individual situations.

Effective Interactions Teachers Should Use and Why

What to Do	Rationale
For any group, including a classroom, to be successful, its members must be unified to accomplish a common goal.	If the students do not unify to help each other accomplish the common goal of academic achievement, the class will usually become dysfunctional.
When a student says or does something that hurts the common purpose, the teacher must address the situation without criticizing the offending student.	Teachers do not help the common purpose by allowing students to criticize others. However, teachers must be aware their criticism of a student is equally damaging. Embarrassing any student undermines the students working for a common purpose.
Students need to be encouraged to promote the success of all other students. Unless all students are working for the common purpose, maximum learning will not occur.	Teachers must show that they care about the success of every student. If students notice that a teacher has given up on one student, the class will no longer be committed to helping each other succeed.
Competition needs to be reduced.	Competition always results in many students losing. Competition against outside groups helps a group unite for the good of the group. However, competition within a group is extremely difficult to manage unless the members voluntarily joined the group for the chance to compete with others. When competition is created between classes, some or even most classes will lose.
Help students develop persistence to work through difficult situations.	Persistence is an essential attribute. Academic excellence will be difficult for some students. Developing a determination to succeed will be essential for maximum results.
Always work to promote cooperation among the students.	Cooperation will encourage students to strive for success. ☞

What to Do	Rationale
Lead by example.	Teachers should exemplify the kind of person they want students to become.
Provide rationales for everything expected of students.	If teachers want students to learn, they must help them understand the reason for the expectations.

Interactions Teachers Should Avoid Using and Why

What Teachers Need to Avoid	Rationale
Never give students an excuse to fail.	When given excuses, students will soon find an excuse for repeatedly failing.

4

Methods for Creating Successful Classrooms

HE MOST INCREDIBLE THING ABOUT CHILDREN is that they are ready-made for learning. If a teacher is prepared to begin at the students' developmental level, children are perfectly built to learn in schools. They come to school in small, varied, and imperfect packages, but with the necessities to learn — human needs. The psychological and survival needs of humans serve as the motivational drive necessary to learn in any possible environment. When teachers learn how to help students meet their needs, they can develop students who are ambitious, cooperative, and outstanding students. Currently, in this country, this is easier than ever before because — with only a few exceptions — children's survival needs are at least minimally met by social programs. When survival needs are satisfied, students are instead driven to satisfy their psychological needs including socialization, avoiding psychological pain, intellectual stimulation, and autonomy.

When we talk to teachers, they often tell us the only problems affecting their class are a few behavioral issues; nevertheless, students would not excel if our methods only provided solutions for behavioral problems. To solve these *and* help students reach their potential, teachers must have a new system for motivating appropriate behavior. This chapter will describe the framework of a positive motivational system and later chapters will detail the application to the behaviors students need to learn.

At the beginning of a school year, teachers will need to learn to adjust their methods for the grade level and type of students they have in class. The first order of business is to develop their students' expectations of success. This is not so much their cognitive as their emotional expectations. While the students' cognition will play a role, all students must develop a positive emotional outlook for the classroom and coming school year. At the kindergarten and primary level this will mean that in just two or three days anxiety is replaced by an eagerness to succeed. Fear of failure gives way to hope of success. The teacher helps students replace their self-doubt with a budding self-confidence. Soon, some students, who dread being rejected by classmates, will begin to feel included and important. Other students, who are terrified of being identified as a failure, will soon realize that they are becoming successful.

Teachers at different grade levels and in various schools will encounter different challenges. Maybe in a suburban school, a second grade teacher can move past this emotional outlook step in a few hours. However, a fourth grade teacher, with a class where most of the students had little success in school for the past three years, will have a steep hill to climb. In essence, every teacher will need to start by ensuring all students develop an optimistic mindset.

Teachers will often say, "I know how to teach students to read, and understand numbers; however, I am not a psychologist. I cannot create a new mindset or change how students feel."

The answer is, "Teachers interact with students every minute of every day. You are, therefore, affecting students at the social, emotional, behavioral, and, cognitive levels; each of these elements interact to influence academic learning." Our job is to help every teacher develop the expertise to use every interaction to develop self-confident students who use all the elements of their mind to excel.

The Motivational Process

Many teachers find themselves bogged down in trying to stop problem behavior. Traditionally, teachers have responded with a consequence or by scolding students for minor disruptions or being off task. All such teacher interactions are designed to stop inappropriate behavior, but fail to develop the appropriate behavior. The secret to developing the classroom environment teachers want is to approach the problem differently. For every inappropriate behavior that ever occurred in a school, a corresponding appropriate behavior represents the lesson to be taught. Instead of using consequences for every problem, a teacher uses specific techniques to develop appropriate behavior.

When Art trains potential teachers and describes his approach to teaching, nearly everyone is enthusiastic. However, one teacher, just three minutes after entering the classroom for the first time, saw a student grab a treasured toy from a second child; a chase and resulting fight ensued. The teacher immediately concluded, "So much for his ridiculous theory." She later said that she was thinking, "The idiot who thought up that idea had never seen a real kid."

She yelled at the students running through the classroom and they stopped and returned to their seats. This teacher had temporarily succeeded. Her anxiety had momentarily gone through the roof; however, as the two students walked back to their seats her anxiety receded. The science of human behavior is a funny thing; teachers are also subject to the same process of learning that affects students. The immediate actions of students can affect teachers' actions. When the students went back to their desks, they taught her to raise her voice. Because of the immediate success, she soon learned to stop disruptive behavior by raising her voice. Those two students had stopped what they were doing: exactly what she wanted. Her response had worked. Inappropriate behavior, however, soon became a nearly constant problem. By yelling at the students the teacher had increased their anxiety and that of all the other students. As humans, the students are motivated to reduce their anxiety, and they have several ways to do just that. They can talk to their friends, run around the classroom, throw things, call the teacher names, or get angry with someone. All of those behaviors will reduce anxiety and consequently the students were soon doing those things and more. The vicious cycle had begun.

The teacher's pain could have been avoided if only Art had poured all of his knowledge and experience into her head before she started; unfortunately, we do not have that technology. After several days, the teacher asked Art, "Is there a way off this merry-go-round that does not involve homicide, suicide, or insanity?" The answer was yes. Following six days of training, the cycle was broken and the students were free to learn.

If a teacher wants students to refrain from certain behaviors, several factors are necessary.

1. Students must understand the rules and how they benefit themselves and others.
2. Students must trust teachers to protect them from injury and psychological pain.
3. Teachers must create success.
4. Teachers must use a positive motivation system that encourages appropriate student behavior.
5. Each group of students must learn to work for the benefit of everyone.

With these conditions present all students can use their prefrontal cortex to inhibit inappropriate behavior.

A teacher does not want to be in a position of stopping misbehavior; instead, teachers want the students to choose to behave appropriately. However, such a scenario requires a unique approach to teaching, and that approach must be consistent with the research into human behavior and neuroscience. The solution is not to punish inappropriate behavior, but to strengthen appropriate behavior.

Individuals do not easily give up on functional responses. A caveman did not quit fishing because a bear chased him away from the river. Humans easily learn to persevere in the face of hardship. Too often in education, coercive teachers become the hardship. As a result, students develop the persistence to endure school, or ridicule the teacher. A difficult lesson for teachers to understand is that students will eliminate their own maladaptive responses when they are driven to learn. We have had teachers complain that they cannot wait for such a process to work; however, the process we describe will start working in just two minutes. In just a few weeks, teachers can have students managing their own behavior.

Using Positive Motivation

For a student or a group of students to master their academic material, they must first learn to behave in ways that promote learning in a group setting. To help students in this process, teachers will need a motivational system. The basic research into the motivation of human behavior was carefully studied decades ago, and the science is still the same. However, the application to education has resulted in behavioral management procedures that have muddled the science almost beyond recognition. As described in Chapter Two, behavioral research showed that any behavior that is immediately followed by a reinforcing stimulus will occur more frequently. Consider an example. When a child is hungry, he remembers that food is kept in the kitchen. The child, therefore, goes to the kitchen. He does not go to the bathroom, bedroom, or shed out back, unless that is where food is kept. Children will both remember where food is kept and engage in the necessary behavior to get it. Finding food was the reinforcing stimulus for remembering where to go and then going to the kitchen. Readers should also understand that the behavior will be learned even if at times children do not find food in the kitchen. Sometimes the caveman did not find apples on the apple tree, but he did not forget how to find the tree. The same brain functions are necessary for remembering information and behaving appropriately.

Students will choose to behave in ways that benefit them, because that is the nature of humans. They may or may not behave in ways that benefit teachers. If teachers want students to behave in ways that make teaching easier, they must be sure that such behavior benefits every student. Getting students willingly to pursue accomplishments is the only realistic path to academic achievement. Teachers only have a few choices for motivating behavior. Only two of the psychological needs we listed have much potential for teaching. Intellectual stimulation is important but cannot be manipulated to strengthen specific behavior. Social approval is the only human need that can be manipulated to motivate student behavior in classrooms. Fortunately, teachers can use social approval to build any behavior that is important to success in school. Chapter Two established the reasons for not using secondary reinforcers.

To apply the motivational methods, teachers must understand different types of behavior. We will classify behaviors into three types: simple, complex, and continuation behaviors. Simple behaviors typically take very little time to complete. A student sitting down in his seat is an example of a simple behavior. However, a student remaining in his seat is a continuation behavior and such behaviors can be maintained for considerable periods. For example, running is a simple behavior that marathon runners continue for hours. Running for more than a few seconds would be considered a continuation behavior. Some behaviors are considered complex because they require chaining several simple behaviors together to do a task. For instance, starting a car is a complex behavior. To start a car one must have a key in one's hand, insert it in the ignition, have one's foot on the brake, the transmission in park, and turn the key to start the engine. Each behavior is a simple behavior, but they must be combined to start a car.

Teachers must understand how to strengthen various types of behaviors. For instance, to reinforce a student for hanging up his backpack (a simple behavior) the reinforcer must occur within a second or two following the behavior. Little, if any benefit, will be realized if a student is reinforced for behaviors that occurred several minutes earlier.

An obvious goal of teachers is to increase the number of correct responses to academic material. For example, a student could answer a verbal question from the teacher; this would be a simple behavior and if he is correct the answer must be reinforced immediately following the response. Because other students can hear the answer, the reinforcer serves a dual purpose. Not only does the particular student need the feedback, but other students also need confirmation on whether the answer is correct. Teachers do not want to fail to reinforce correct answers, because to do so would leave several students confused. Acknowledging verbal answers as correct is necessary for academic development.

More often a problem arises when students give incorrect answers that other students see or hear. Some care must be taken to reduce the negative effect on the student who gave the incorrect answer to a teacher's question in front of the group or students will start dreading being asked questions. For an incorrect answer, the teacher should avoid saying the answer was wrong. We advise teachers immediately to ask the same question to another student. If necessary, we would advise teachers to ask the question to two or three students in succession. When the question is answered correctly, the teacher should acknowledge the correct answer. Following the acknowledgment of the correct answer, the teacher wants every student who answered incorrectly to answer correctly. Every student who participated needs to answer the question correctly and get the teacher's recognition for that. Sometimes teachers will need to give the correct answer to a student and immediately have the student repeat it. Learning is a result of correct answers being reinforced. Teachers can get students to relish the opportunities to show what they know.

The situation is a little different when a student has written an incorrect answer on the board and other students are watching to see if it is correct. In these instances, we would suggest the teacher respond in one of two ways. First, the teacher can help the student answer correctly. When the answer is correct she then gives her verbal recognition of the correct answer. As a second alternative, a teacher could have the first student step aside and invite another student to show the correct answer. However, she must also get the first student to get the correct answer so it can be reinforced. If the question were to identify the subject of a sentence, this will work. If however, the question was to work a long division problem, the other students might get bored. In instances where a teacher wants a student to show a complex solution, she would be well advised to pick a student who can not only get the correct answer but also explain the process. This is not a preferred situation for a student who is expected to have difficulty.

A long division problem is a complex behavior that requires a series of simple and continuation behaviors to complete. Presumably, to work such a problem a student would first need to sit and pick up a pencil. These are both simple behaviors. However, the student will need to continue holding the pencil and remain seated. These are continuation behaviors. To finish the problem, the student will need to repeat a series of steps including multiplication, subtraction, and writing numbers in the correct spot. While each of these responses are simple behaviors, they must be chained together in an exact order to get the correct answer. The process for teaching complex behaviors is to reinforce each simple behavior and reinforce their sequencing. Some students will require considerable practice and many reinforcers to learn complex behaviors.

Teaching students to string together several complex behaviors is more difficult. (Writing a paragraph would be an example.) Even so, the process is the same. Any such task would require a teacher repeatedly to explain what the students need to do, in what order, and the importance of the task. However, explaining everything to students would only be part of developing highly complex behavior. Such an endeavor, at the elementary school level, will take practice and dozens of reinforcers during every practice period. The fact that a few students could learn to do the process quickly is of little significance. Teachers cannot meet their academic goals unless all students are successful.

However, establishing continuation behaviors requires a different reinforcement process. We will describe an example of a student continuing to work on a seatwork assignment. When students are left to set their own work habits, some students will work one problem, answer one question, or even write a letter or two and stop. Students cannot become successful if they stop to daydream every few moments. Fortunately, a specific teaching process can keep all students working. Continuation behaviors must be reinforced while the behavior is occurring; they cannot be strengthened after the student has stopped the behavior. When a student stops his work, he has engaged in the simple behavior of stopping. A reinforcer delivered even one tenth of one second after the student stopped work would reinforce the student for stopping his work. The reinforcer must be delivered while the student is working. This is another example where teachers may consider it inconvenient that human beings were built this way. Nevertheless, the specifics mentioned above describe the nature of human learning, and teachers must use a process constructed on the principles of learning.

During seatwork, students continue their work and generate both correct and incorrect answers. By walking around the classroom and looking over students' shoulders while they are working, teachers can find several instances of correct responses. Students can be reinforced for continuing to work and for their correct answers. During periods of seatwork, teachers should move around the room randomly and check the students' work. When a teacher finds correct answers she praises the work and marks the item as correct. However, for incorrect answers we advise teachers to mark the item as needing to be corrected. Students should correct or ask the teacher for help with issues that she notices during seatwork assignments. The quicker the mistake can be corrected the better for learning. The teacher will go back and check as many of the corrections as possible during that seatwork session. One of our favorite teachers has a remarkable response when a student says, "Oh, I got that wrong." She answers, "No, you don't have it correct yet." The development of seatwork will be described more fully in Chapter Six.

Besides academic responses, thousands of other behaviors occur in a classroom every day. As all teachers know, some behaviors help produce a successful learning environment and some are counterproductive. Helping students build a repertoire of constructive behaviors is the foundation of them achieving to the limits of their potential. Distinguishing between productive and nonproductive responses must happen quickly and teachers may find it difficult to classify each behavior instantly. To help new teachers with this challenge, Art has his teachers list how they want students to behave in all situations. This exercise helps teachers envision how they want students to behave and helps them instantly recognize such behavior.

We often find teachers wish they could reinforce behavior that occurred earlier. Frequently, we have found it necessary to repeat ourselves on the issue of not trying to reinforce behaviors several minutes after they occur. If a teacher wants to increase the consistency of students walking into class, hanging up coats and backpacks, and walking to their seats, she must reinforce many instances of each behavior. Those behaviors must be reinforced immediately. However, this brings us to a point that is fortunate for teachers. Every instance of the behavior does not have to be reinforced for a student to learn. Reinforcing the behavior for several students every morning for a few days might be enough to establish the behavior. However, once the behaviors are established, reinforcing a few instances of the behaviors every few days would be necessary to maintain them. Of course, a teacher has a larger problem, because she is not only trying to teach 25 or more students to hang up their backpacks, but also dozens of other academic and deportment-type behaviors. (By "deportment-type" we are referring to the demeanor or manner in which students conduct themselves.) By reinforcing various behaviors of several students throughout each day for several days, most students will learn to behave appropriately. Once many students are behaving consistently, other students will learn quickly. Within just a few weeks the culture (the typical behavior of students) does most of the work.

Nevertheless, students may discontinue behaviors that are not reinforced. Consistent with the science of human behavior, actions that are not reinforced will be discontinued in that setting. When a teacher seldom reinforces certain behaviors or certain behaviors of some students, she should not be surprised if those students discontinue the behavior. However, once a behavior is well learned, only occasional instances of the behavior need to be reinforced to maintain the response. Unfortunately, if a teacher is going to insist on punishing students for failing to comply with expectations, she should expect the problem of building appropriate behavior to take much longer. When even occasional consequences are used, the number of reinforcers and the time necessary to develop appropriate behavior may become nearly impossible. This will be more obvious in group situations than at home with one or two children. We are sometimes asked, "If students discontinue behaviors that are not reinforced, shouldn't they also discontinue punished behaviors?" As stated earlier, punishment motivates students to avoid the setting. When the punitive situation cannot be avoided, students often respond by becoming defiant or even develop a resistance to learn what is being taught.

Another common misconception is that simply telling a student to hang up his backpack should result in the student learning the behavior. While telling students what is expected of them is important, teachers should not expect instructions to replace the requirement of reinforcing the behavior. Reinforcing behavior should be considered an essential part of getting behavior to continue. When the productive behavior stops, the reason is usually that the behavior is not being reinforced. Every teacher who has learned this methodology has had to take responsibility for students failing because she was not using enough reinforcers. Teachers will find this to be a humbling experience.

The power of social approval is increased by using specific descriptions of the behavior. Saying to a student, "Good job," is of little value.

Such a statement might serve as a reinforcer for the behavior that occurred immediately before the words were spoken. However, the student was most likely doing several things. If he was working at his seat, he was probably sitting. He might have been holding a pencil and looking at his paper. He could be talking to himself or tapping his foot. The question is which behavior did the teacher want to reinforce? Was she impressed with how much work he had accomplished? Was it the neatness of his paper that caught her attention? The teacher needs to say exactly what it is that impresses her. She could say, "Wow! You are almost done. Good work." Such a statement would likely serve as a reinforcer for working quickly. If a behavior is not successful in generating a reinforcing stimulus, the behavior eventually will be discontinued. When teachers try to teach without reinforcing student behavior, they unknowingly reduce the strength of important behavior. Especially in the elementary grades the behaviors necessary for success will be weak. Failure to reinforce important behaviors will result in some students failing to learn.

Fundamental Three states: "Anything that affects one student affects every student." This suggests another benefit of praising students. When a student is reinforced for hanging up his backpack and other students hear the teacher thank him, many students will be affected and it will be positive. Specific praise statements frequently have a suggestive influence on other students. Some students, after hearing a teacher praise other students for hanging up their backpacks, will turn around and hang up their own. The praise suggested or pointed out to other students, how to get the teacher's attention. The teacher could then praise those students for hanging up their backpacks. While some backpacks may not get hung up on the first three days, in just a few days most will be hung up. If some students do not learn quickly to follow the rules, other techniques are available. Within just a few weeks, for kindergarten and the primary grades, all students should nearly always be following the rules. Students will soon come to behave appropriately because that is what is appreciated by the teacher. However, another factor can help improve the way students behave: when teachers are careful to describe the rationale for all appropriate behavior, students will soon understand the importance of everything expected of them. Within just a few weeks, as they begin to be more successful they willingly manage their behavior for the benefit of everyone. Nevertheless, they are still children and will sometimes forget or try to get by with less effort. However, the methods we describe give teachers the skills to correct anything that goes wrong.

An important issue in using social approval is that it must be genuine. Teachers must be sincere when they praise student behavior. If they are not sincere, their praise will sound phony and will have less beneficial effect. The best way to ensure genuine statements is for teachers to watch for those behaviors they truly admire. If a teacher, in fact, admires the student's work, her words will not be phony — but therein lies a trap. Teachers must learn to admire the little things that contribute to students excelling in school. For instance, keeping numbers in the correct columns is important in basic math. Teachers cannot withhold praise until a student extracts the square root of a three-digit number. All advanced skills are dependent on learning the simple skills first.

Some teachers will feel awkward when they begin praising students. Fortunately, that is not a fatal flaw. Art has had hundreds of teachers force their way through that period and within several days their praises become natural. Fortunately, no harm will come to students because of a few forced praise statements.

When a teacher finds positive ways to motivate appropriate behavior, students have no reason to mistrust her. In the absence of negative consequences, students are not at risk of being shamed in front of their peers. They will quickly learn to approach every new expectation without fear. The relationship between a teacher and students will be strengthened each day. When teachers use positive procedures for building appropriate behavior, they will find many positive ripples throughout the group.

Distributing Praise

Teachers must be careful, every day, to distribute their praise equally across all students. Unlike tangible reinforcers such as stickers, school tokens, or small toys, praise statements cannot be tallied at the end of the day. As a result, the problem of students resenting other students for getting more attention is reduced. If a teacher is close to achieving an equal distribution of praise, the process will work. However, if a few students get most of the praise, other students will recognize the inequity and begin acting out. They will find a way to get their share of attention even if it is negative. Some students need more praise than others; therefore, effective teachers will give them a little more attention. Because those students who need the least amount of attention to be on task will not miss what they do not need, minor inequities are not a problem. If, however, a teacher finds herself remembering that she needs to praise, she must be careful not to look at the same students each time. Some students usually behave as they are expected to. Teachers can count on them to work and behave appropriately. Teachers may fall into the trap of praising these students more often; however, this will create a new problem. Those students who need the most help in building productive classroom behavior will be getting the least recognition. The result will be that those students who cannot match the best students will find a way to demand attention or act out their frustration.

Praise must also be equally distributed across time. If a teacher praises at the beginning of the school day, but fails to praise in the afternoon, she will teach the students to only work in the mornings. They will become as lazy as the teacher, who will find there are no shortcuts in the distribution of praise.

When Art observes teachers who are having problems with their class, he often finds one of two problems. The teacher may not be using enough praise or is failing to distribute her approval equally. This problem has the potential of becoming a circular trap. Those students who most need the teacher's approval are seldom on task so they have fewer opportunities to learn the necessary behavior. Because they get less attention for appropriate behavior, they will behave appropriately less often. The trap has closed. The only way out requires the methods to be used more precisely. Sometimes it takes several days of observation and feedback from a supervisor to break the cycle.

Differential Social Attention: The Most Important Process

Teachers are faced with a thousand things to do and one of those is to bring order to a complicated environment. Typically a teacher has 20 to 30 students and some will behave perfectly most of the time while others will be off task or disruptive. At any given moment, many behaviors are happening simultaneously. Some students are behaving exactly as expected, while others are making life miserable for the teacher and other students. Teachers cannot possibly deal with everything that is happening in a classroom. In fact, teachers can address much less than ten percent of classroom behavior. That leaves the teacher with no alternative except to ignore more than 90 percent of what happens. This does not need to be disconcerting, but it does define how classroom teaching must be practiced. A teacher cannot reinforce every appropriate behavior and she cannot possibly chase every misbehavior. Teachers cannot tell each student everything he needs to do, or correct students every time they misbehave. Readers should not construe this to mean that expectations must be lowered. Concurrent with the new methods, standards for student behavior and academic achievement can be raised. Teachers have an alternate method of developing and maintaining learning-related behavior in students. This methodology, which we have now partially described, is based on what is and is not possible in classrooms.

Social approval immediately following appropriate student behavior is a major factor in that process. However, because teachers cannot attend to everything that is happening in a classroom, teachers must find strategic ways to decide how they will direct their attention. Fortunately, the most effective process for teaching involves the teacher selectively directing and withholding her attention based on student behavior. One way to get students to stop behaving inappropriately is to reduce the attention to misbehavior. While a teacher does not control everything that is happening in a classroom, she can withhold her attention to inappropriate behavior. By withholding her attention to inappropriate, but not dangerous, behavior, the ignored behavior will weaken. Since attending to everything that happens in a classroom is impossible, this is the only viable way for teachers to manage classroom behavior. This process is called *differential social attention*. Differential social attention is the most important process available to teachers.

Teachers will say to us, "But you don't understand. All of this bad behavior must be stopped before I can even think about the things you suggest." The behavior needs to stop, but the problems will get worse if the methods used are coercive. Remember, for every inappropriate behavior, the teacher needs to strengthen the corresponding appropriate behavior. If some students are out of their seats, the teacher needs to find a student or two who are in their seats and praise them. When some students are being noisy, she needs to find other students who are being quiet. The process of differential social attention will strengthen the appropriate behaviors and weaken the inappropriate ones. If this process is correctly and consistently used for a few weeks, nearly every student will be following classroom rules most of the time.

The concept is applied the same way to individual students. The teacher would direct her attention to any given student when he is behaving appropriately and withhold her attention for inappropriate behavior. When a student changes from behaving inappropriately to appropriately, the teacher will point out his appropriate behavior. For instance, if a teacher noticed Josh did not hang up his backpack, she would praise those who remembered. If Josh then turns around and hangs up his backpack, she needs to recognize his behavior. (Her attention was differentially distributed based on his behavior.) Hanging up a backpack is a case of a simple behavior and would need to be recognized immediately. However, for a student returning to a seatwork assignment, the situation is different. Seatwork is a continuation behavior; therefore, she would delay her praise for a few seconds. A continuation behavior must be reinforced while it is continuing, therefore the delay.

At this point we feel obliged to point out that a problem is never ignored. When we recommend differential social attention, we are suggesting that an instance of the behavior be ignored for that student. However, the authors would never recommend that an ongoing problem be ignored. For instance, if a student is out of his seat the teacher will most likely want to ignore that single instance of the behavior. However, if one student is out of his seat on one occasion, the teacher can be sure that he will be out of his seat on other occasions and other students will follow his lead. Teachers must have other alternatives for teaching students to stay in their seats. These cannot be techniques whose implementation takes hours to design and prepare. Instead, we offer extremely powerful techniques designed to get students to take greater responsibility for their own behavior. Once a teacher learns the methodology, she can devise the plan in a few seconds and never miss a minute of teaching. The plan may be to continue differential social attention or she might decide to make her expectations more clear. Perhaps the plan would be to increase her praise rates or revisit having students practice the appropriate behavior. Any of these plans might be effective in reducing inappropriate behavior or in improving the behavior of other students. Improving the behavior of the class as a whole would improve the classroom culture. The improved culture might help the targeted student. Perhaps the teacher could decide to increase her diligence and watch more closely for good behavior from that student. If she can catch him being good, and reinforce such behavior more often, his overall behavior would improve. However, she might decide that she must create better behavior by talking directly to him about how he needs to behave, and the reason for appropriate behavior. If by talking to him, she creates better behavior for even a few minutes, she will have more opportunities to reinforce the appropriate behavior.

Some readers may be tempted to disregard these suggestions as too weak to address the problems they encounter. In our experience, teachers proficient in these methods never need to call for an IEP meeting for behavior problems. When all teachers are proficient in the methods we advocate, IEPs for behavioral issues would almost never be needed. More options are described in Chapters Five and Seven.

For education to be effective, students must learn to work together and become independently responsible for much of their learning. Because teachers can only attend to less than ten percent of what happens in their classroom, they must get students to take considerable responsibility for themselves and each other. Teachers will, therefore, need to use positive motivation to build behaviors that benefit learning. They must also motivate students to maintain such behavior. Teachers must establish compliance but they must remember that cooperation is more important in developing responsible independence than compliance.

For example, Vera Knoll had 27 students in her fourth grade class. Art sat in on a morning in early September. The school was in the most difficult section of a large city. She had just told the students to take out their journals and write about the terrible weather the city had been having. Several students were not following her instructions. Some students were out of their seats. Many students were talking and laughing with other students. He counted six students who were following instructions. Vera immediately praised each of those students for beginning work on their journals. Her praises were loud enough for everyone to hear. A moment later, she again praised each of those students. Two girls quit talking and got out their journals. Vera immediately praised those two girls for beginning work. Again she praised each of the original six students for continuing to work. Then she praised the two girls for continuing to work. She had not said anything to the students who were not working. By this point about two minutes had elapsed since her instruction to the class. She had already used 20 praise statements directed to those who were working. Soon after that, three more students started working. At that point she had 11 of the 27 students working. Vera did not show the slightest frustration with those students who were not working. She continued to praise students for working. However, by this point she was moving around the room. She would stop and read what a student had written. Some of her comments were about what she had read. She was still praising at a very high rate, but she was also instructing students about their writing. Art did an on-task count six minutes following the initial instruction. Nineteen of the students were on task. Vera continued directing her praise and attention to those students who were working. After 12 minutes 21 of the students had started working. At any given moment about 65 to 75 percent of the students were working. The criteria would be always to have at least 80 percent of the students on task, but that would take a few weeks to accomplish. This teacher had gotten the students working without any consequences, reminders, or threats. The students had exercised their autonomy and chosen to work. Nearly every student had inhibited the temptation to talk to friends. Once they started working, reinforcers would strengthen work-related behaviors. Because the students had initiated their work, they had made a significant step to becoming self-disciplined.

Students Soliciting Praise

A difficulty teachers will face from time to time is a student soliciting praise; teachers do not want students begging for attention. Consider the following example. Dan Jacobs praised a student for hanging up his coat. Immediately Cathy said, "Mr. Jacobs, I hung up my coat too."

Dan responded, "We don't beg for recognition. That is not the way to earn the admiration of others." These words were not said directly to Cathy, instead they were an indirect reference to what Cathy said.

He turned and said to Mari, "Thank you for walking directly to your seat. I appreciate that. Brandon remembered to get his homework out of his backpack." Dan had described the behavior he expected and withheld his attention to unwanted behavior. Nevertheless, the following day he encountered another similar situation. After hearing Dan praise another student, Loni said, "Mr. Jacobs, look at my paper. It's better than hers." In this instance, however, Dan ignored the attempt to solicit praise. He said nothing to Loni, and he did not use an indirect reference to the statement. He simply continued developing the behaviors he wanted the students to exemplify. Dan Jacobs was an effective teacher and had very few such behaviors in his class. Such comments from students are better corrected without the use of consequences. Differential social attention will solve the problem; however, explaining to students that there are some behaviors that are not admired might be necessary.

Every student is always doing something. Remember, a teacher cannot attend to all behavior in a classroom and fortunately does not need to. The reason differential social attention is perfect in classrooms is because students, in anticipation of a teacher's recognition, will correct their own behavior. Behaviors continue though they are not reinforced every time they occur. People continue to go fishing though sometimes they do not catch any fish. In fact, those behaviors that achieve the desired outcome at unpredictable times become the strongest. The fact that a teacher cannot be perfect in applying differential social attention actually improves the results. No other process available to teachers allows them to strengthen appropriate behavior and weaken inappropriate behavior in the time available. Teachers can use differential social attention to achieve incredible results. They need not worry which students are assigned to their classroom because they will succeed with even the most difficult. Only a few skills are necessary to create the difference between disappointing results and all students excelling.

One of the most predictable things about groups is that, when teachers explain how they want students to behave, some students will attempt to behave as the teacher wants them to. This means that at the beginning of the day some students will, within seconds, be behaving according to the teacher's wishes. As a result, teachers can begin reinforcing appropriate behavior immediately. With each social reinforcer, appropriate behavior will be strengthened for at least one student. The third fundamental (anything that affects one student will affect all students) assures that some additional students will benefit from the positive interaction. Teachers must remember to ignore those behaviors that are counterproductive to the goals of the class. A teacher who has withheld her attention from nonproductive behavior has also affected all students. In just a few minutes, the teacher has had a triple influence on student behavior: she has reinforced appropriate behavior, ignored inappropriate behavior, and other students benefited from seeing the interactions.

Teachers will find it necessary to maintain high rates of social approval for at least several weeks. However, the number of weeks is not the variable that determines when the rate of social approval can be decreased. Eventually, teachers can reduce the frequency of praise when student behavior warrants the reduction. We have known teachers who have had to maintain high rates of praise for a few months. In most years, Mrs. Williams can reduce her rate of praise within a few weeks. Nevertheless, teachers must continue to use enough social approval to maintain appropriate behavior. The deportment-type and learning-related behavior of students determine what needs to be done.

Teachers frequently argue that they cannot ignore all misbehavior. We are not advocating that teachers ignore behavior that is dangerous or destructive. Students will sometimes behave in ways that would endanger their own safety or others'. Teachers cannot ignore safety concerns; consequently they must intervene to stop dangerous behavior. The same would go for many destructive behaviors. This book will address interventions for extreme behavior in Chapter Eight; however, many behavior issues are minor. A student being out of his seat, talking to another student, or paying no attention to the teacher, represent examples of behavior that do not endanger anyone's safety. Differential social attention will increase opposite behaviors and consequently, target behaviors are reduced. Some readers may notice we used the phrase "reducing the frequency" of the inappropriate behavior as opposed to "extinguishing" the behavior, which is the standard psychological terminology. We are not partial to the phrase "extinguishing behavior" because the behaviors are not extinguished as much as they are replaced with behaviors that are being reinforced. To reach his goals a student must cognitively inhibit some responses. Despite the process used to reduce inappropriate behavior, the behaviors will remain in the student's repertoire. Short of removing the child's brain, one cannot extinguish unwanted behavior; however, students will suppress behaviors that are not proving beneficial in the current environment.

Humans must retain the potential for bringing particular behaviors back when they again find themselves in an environment where such behavior is accepted, necessary, or results in need satisfaction. Disruptive and nonproductive behaviors can reemerge in subsequent years if such behaviors are adaptive to the environment. Nothing can be done to delete a behavior from a student's memory. Students will never forget how to behave in environments that encourage disruptive and irresponsible behavior. The only reasonable choice is to get students to choose responsible behaviors for any setting teachers have control over. Professionals should understand that children will always adjust their behavior to the current situation. However, when students find that responsible behavior benefits them year after year, they do not easily switch back to the old patterns they used previously.

Problem Behavior

We have found that many professionals, including educators, are reluctant to accept that problem behavior cannot be fixed forever. People may better understand this when they accept that no one can make a child do anything. When teachers use effective methods students willingly adopt appropriate behavior. However, the use of coercive methods will likely fail. If a student refused to sit, how could a teacher make him sit? He might sit if asked or bribed. He might sit if threatened, but it is his choice. Even if someone pointed a gun to his head, the choice would still be his. Someone could shove him into a chair; because of the violence, the student might choose to remain there. However, his behavior is his choice.

Educators must accept that education involves getting students to voluntarily adopt behaviors that will help them excel. Behavior can be coerced for a single instance or even to continue for a few minutes, but a person who is coerced into a response never maintains such behavior over the long term. Coercion may also create an emotional response to a situation where teachers want reason to prevail. The use of coercion is a momentary answer to a problem that requires a long-term solution. Because teachers want appropriate behavior to continue, they must find effective ways to reinforce those behaviors. However, we must admit that we have seen an occasional teacher who could coerce a student into a response, and immediately use enough social reinforcers over the next several days that the appropriate behavior became well established.

Competing Reinforcers

Another difficulty teachers will encounter is that some behaviors of students are self-reinforcing. For example, the need to move can motivate a child's behavior. While most of us eventually learn to control that need and satisfy it at scheduled times, young students may not have the same self-restraint. Being out of their seat and running around the classroom may feel really good, because muscle movement serves as the reinforcer.

The following example shows how Cari handled this problem. On a September morning about two weeks into the school year, 22 of her 24 students had done very well at remaining in their seats. Two boys had been out of their seats for about two minutes. Her efforts, to that point, had not been successful. She guessed it would take much work to get them to sit and stay seated. They were enjoying themselves and distracting other students. The students being out of their seats for a few minutes and the corresponding distraction to other students were not going to destroy academic achievement for a year. Nevertheless, she needed to address the issue immediately. She praised four students for being seated, but did not direct any attention to the two boys who did not even notice. She adjusted her praise statements.

Cari said, "Heather is working so hard, I know it gets tiring being in your seat so long, but that is the way we learn. Marti is working away, she is determined to learn everything she can. Kevin won't give in to the temptation to quit working. He just keeps plugging away."

Cari continued this process for several minutes, but neither of the boys paid any attention. The differential social attention that would most often work like magic was not affecting these boys. She decided to use an alternate method to get the boys started working. Once she could get them to begin, she would use differential social attention to keep them working. Cari broke for recess a few minutes early and directed the students to play tag. She got those two, Matt and Will, to help her organize the game. The goal was to keep them running for the entire 15 minutes. Several times during the 15 minutes she urged the student who was "it" to try to catch Matt or Will. By the end of recess she had the students tired out.

When they came in, she took both Matt and Will by the hand and led them to the carpet area. She did not admonish them or place any demands on them. Nevertheless, she needed to get appropriate behavior to occur and reinforce that behavior. Over the previous few days both boys had shown interest in listening to stories. Cari decided to read a story. By having Matt sit on one side of her and Will on the other side, she kept everyone including Matt and Will engaged in the story. She expressed her admiration to many students for sitting and listening. Matt and Will got a few extra praises for paying attention. As always, she asked many questions regarding the story and directed a few of those questions to Matt and Will. They were praised for their correct answers and paying attention. She made a point to tell each of them that they were on their way to becoming smart. By creating a situation where the behavior she wanted would occur, she could reinforce the appropriate behavior.

After the story, she had the students go back to their seats to work on another seatwork assignment. However, this time she led Matt and Will to their seats and got them started working. Going back to seatwork was a deviation from her planned schedule, but she needed the boys to be successful working in their seats. Fortunately, the boy's seats were close to each other; she was seldom more than a couple steps from either boy so her physical presence would help keep them working. The intent was for the boys to be successful at a seatwork assignment even if only for a few minutes. They were praised for picking up their pencils, staying in their seats, keeping their pencils in their hands, and writing their letters. Other students were also being praised. During the next several minutes, she praised students' work-related behavior more than 50 times. The high rate allowed her to get nearly a dozen approval statements to Matt and Will without the other students feeling left out. (It should be noted that this rate of praise was only a little higher than she would normally use so early in the school year.) In about three weeks, these boys were approximating the on-task levels expected of beginning kindergarten students. After getting the students started working, the process was simple; she used differential social attention to maintain their behavior.

As described earlier, the third fundamental (anything that affects one student affects everyone) means that teachers can use praise to have a suggestive influence on disruptive students. By praising students for staying in their seats, a student who is out of his seat might catch on that he too could get the teacher's approval by being in his seat. That is a good use of differential social approval. However, this process can be so effective that it creates another trap. The greatest likelihood of seeing off-task behavior is at times when a teacher has slacked off in the use of differential social attention, and even the best teachers will slack off sometimes. In these instances, teachers will often notice a student who is not engaged in productive work and realize her mistake. She then renews her efforts and the process works exactly like it is supposed to work; the student goes back to work. However, the teacher has inadvertently set a trap for herself. If the targeted student returns to work, the teacher might again slack off. If so, she just walked into her own snare. In just a few such instances, students will realize that the best way to turn on the spigot is to quit working. The solution is for teachers to be careful and rarely slack off. This does not mean teachers must praise at the rate of five praises per minute forever, but it does mean she must be sensitive to the students who are working and what is happening in the class. Excellent student work habits can be maintained with lower rates of praise, unless the praise rates drop off for extended periods. The student's behavior will dictate how the teacher uses the process, but teachers should understand that no matter what mistake a teacher makes, she can correct it.

Other self-reinforcing activities may require other interventions. Students might find playing with toys from home to be more fun than listening to a teacher. In these instances, teachers will simply want to take the toy away and return it later. Teachers will also want to have a rule against students bringing snacks or drinks into class. Competing with a candy bar might be impossible. Some teachers make a rule that any snacks brought into class will be taken away and disposed of, or given to charity.

The Teacher-Student Relationship

Art has spent the last several years of his career helping young children who have very serious mental health issues. Most professionals, including Art, who have worked in the mental health field describe the professional-patient relationship to be a primary agent of change. A similar argument could be made regarding the importance of the teacher-student relationship. However, in classrooms teachers encounter a bit of a paradox. The relationship is important to helping students thrive. But, because of the nature of classrooms, teachers must make giant strides in developing a relationship with every student while working with an entire classroom full of students. As a result, the relationship becomes a secondary agent of change. Interactions that create universal trust, success, greater self-confidence, and a functional group are the initial agents. Most typically, teachers should maximize their efforts during the first two or three days to develop the trust that is the foundation of any relationship. However, unlike a therapist, teachers must accomplish this with each student in a classroom of 20 to 30 students. Teachers have, at most, a few moments of individual time with each student, with all of other students present. Many readers might consider this an incredible disadvantage to teachers. With the correct methodology, though, teachers will find that a classroom full of students is an extraordinary advantage in building constructive relationships with students. After all, in just minutes every student will notice some student developing a budding connection with the teacher.

Readers will remember that all students have a built-in need to be connected with others. Every student wants to be accepted by the other students and admired by the teacher. However, some students, especially in preschool and the primary grades, do not know how to go about making friends. They need help in becoming a constructive member of a functional group. Some students will invariably confuse socialization with being noticed by other students or with dominating the teacher's time. Teachers are therefore faced with a two-part problem. First, they must develop the trust of every student, and second, they must teach students the behaviors necessary to build effective relationships.

We have already described much of what is necessary for students to trust teachers. Every student must be treated with respect and see all other students treated with respect. Teachers will accomplish much of this by setting expectations and using positive procedures to help students become successful. The second issue is to help students learn how to be successful members of a group. Because some students have trouble regulating their emotions, delaying gratification, or inhibiting their need to move, they will behave in ways that sabotage their own goals. We cannot describe everything in this chapter; however, teachers can use the methods described thus far to help students be successful. Helping most students get off to a good start can happen in just a few days.

Some students are very difficult to reach and a one-on-one process for developing the relationship might be necessary. Following is how this was accomplished with one difficult student. Jonathon had been brought to a therapeutic preschool for an assessment to see if he would qualify for the program. He was five years old and currently in his twelfth foster home. Most of the foster placements since he was two years old were disrupted because of his extreme behavioral problems. When Art met him he was living in a therapeutic foster home, but was in serious danger of being removed from that home as well. Recently, his behavior had been nearly intolerable. He had broken a lamp, hurt the family dog, and put poop in his foster parents' bed.

On the day of his assessment, teachers were having difficulty establishing a relationship. Three previous staff members had failed to connect with him. They asked Art to bail them out. Every employee had seen Art succeed at connecting with difficult children, but Jonathon presented exceptional difficulties and Art eventually got help from another teacher. Jonathon would not look at adults, used single word answers, and stayed as far from adults as possible. When Art asked him if he wanted to play basketball, he answered, "Yes." They went out to the basketball hoop, he took the ball and shot it once, and then ran to the far side of the playground. Jonathon let Art approach him, but when Art offered to push him on the swings he ran back to the other side of the playground. For Jonathon, the playground was a perfect place to avoid adult contact. Dr. Willans called inside to Rachel, a seasoned teacher, and told her to meet them in the small hallway by the restroom. With gentleness and empathy, but no coercion, Jonathon took Art's hand and they walked to the hallway. Rachel stood between Jonathon and the restroom and Art stopped at the entrance to the hallway. It was Rachel's turn. She looked at Jonathon and said, "Hi, Jonathon." Jonathon did not answer and did not look at her.

Rachel said, "Sometimes I just feel like stomping my foot." She stomped her foot. She added, "You probably don't like to stomp your foot." Jonathon glanced up for a second. Rachel stomped her foot two more times and said, "I can't stomp my foot very hard. I should get someone to teach me how." Jonathon smiled for the first time that morning and stomped his foot.

Rachel got a surprised look on her face and exclaimed, "You stomped your foot so hard your shoe lit up." Jonathon laughed. "How did you do that? Do my shoes light up?" She stomped her foot three more times and asked, "Did my shoes light up?"

Jonathon laughed and said, "Your shoes don't have lights."

Rachel asked, "How did you put lights in your shoes?"

Jonathon laughed again.

One technique in relating to children is playfulness. Children respond very well to teachers who can have fun. Rachel and Jonathon were now friends. The first order of education had been accomplished — he could trust one teacher. From that beginning, everything he would need in this program was possible. He attended the therapeutic preschool and while he was difficult at times, he was very successful in the program. He remained in the same therapeutic foster home. At the end of the year, he was ready for a regular first grade classroom. The relationship that started with Rachel's connection was part of the reason for his success.

Application in Upper Grades

Applying these methods will be only slightly different with older students. Preschool children need to learn to trace letters, how to hold their pencil, and to color in the lines. These tasks are seldom the issue with sixth grade students. Although, with any age of students, teachers must notice what is standing in the way of excellence. If a sixth grader does not know how to find the right page in his book, the teacher will need to address the issue. More often older students need to learn to read silently, compose a paragraph, and answer word problems. With older students, teachers will not need to give as much attention to students remaining seated; however, every student is different. Classes are different from year to year; therefore, teachers must make adjustments based on the needs of their students.

Another adjustment with older students is that the praise terminology can often be omitted. With older students, teachers may not need to include terms like "good job" or "nice work" into the specific description of what the student is doing. With younger students, teachers are more nurturing, and use lots of direct praise statements. However, even with kindergarten students many teachers will find it effective to omit the compliment and just describe the work being done. For instance instead of saying, "Great, you are working hard," she might instead say, "Ty is working hard." As students develop good work habits, teachers will find the recognition is sufficient to strengthen specific behaviors. These are seldom major issues in training teachers who are new to our methods but experienced in the upper grades. They usually know how to communicate with their students.

Reading to Students

We have encountered teachers who, when reading to students, would lose their attention. However, we find more teachers understand and use the correct process than was the case several years ago.

We will examine an example of Jana Cronin reading to her kindergarten students. This is the same teacher readers met as a young kindergarten teacher and a cheerleading coach before she was married.

Jana: "The Night Before Christmas
Twas the night before Christmas
when all through the house
Not a creature was stirring not even a mouse."

She stopped and asked, "Who knows when Christmas is?" Two hands went up. Mrs. Cronin said, "Brandon when is Christmas?"

Brandon answered, "Soon."

Jana said, "That's right. Does anyone know what day is Christmas?"

Lana raised her hand, but volunteered without being called on. "It's Dec. 25."

Jana replied, "That's right, Christmas is Dec. 25." She continued, "The story mentioned that, 'Not a creature was stirring.' What's a creature?"

No one answered.

She waited. Then she said, "Does anyone know what a creature is?" Still no one responded, so Jana read the first three lines again and asked, "What do you think a creature is?"

Again Jana waited and gave students a chance to think. Then she praised Brandon and Jared for their attention.

Lana eventually said, "I think it is a mouse or something."

"Good listening," Jana said. "Creature is a big word for an animal, a bird, or even a bug. Jared what does creature mean?"

Jared answered, "It means a bug or animal."

Jana said, "Good. You were listening. A creature is anything that is alive that can move around." She continued reading, "The stockings were hung by the chimney with care, in hopes that St. Nicholas soon would be there." Then she asked, "How many of you hang stockings at Christmas?"

Two or three students answered simultaneously, "I do."

Michael said, "We don't have Christmas."

Jana spoke up. "Some people celebrate Christmas and some people don't. It's okay."

Lana asked Michael, "Why not?"

Jana quickly asked, "Michael, do you want to answer that?"

Michael answered, "Momma said it's because we don't celebrate birthdays."

Jana said, "Yes, Christmas is the birthday of Jesus. Is there anyone else who doesn't celebrate Christmas?" No one raised their hand.

Michael asked, "Do you celebrate Christmas, Mrs. Cronin?"

Jana answered, "Yes we do." She continued, "People believe different things, but it is important we learn about each other and learn to accept others and what they believe."

The story continued much the same way for half an hour. During that time she included everyone in the conversation. They did not get through the story but Michael asked if she would finish it. Jana quickly read the remainder of the story. It had turned into a lesson about Christmas, vocabulary, and personal preferences. She revealed things about herself, and students revealed things about themselves. Students learned to listen to the teacher and to each other. They practiced answering questions. She had to be patient and give young students time to think before they could answer questions. She helped students be patient with each other and praised them for listening, sitting still, and being respectful of each other.

Developing Attributes

Another issue for teachers is that only specific behaviors can be identified and therefore strengthened with reinforcers. A class of behavior cannot directly be strengthened. Kindness is a class of behaviors; therefore, the only way to develop kindness is to reinforce specific examples. If a teacher wants students to become more kind to other students, she can work on that problem by finding little acts of kindness. She could start with a discussion of how to be kind to others. Following such a discussion, she would notice some examples of kind behavior and reinforce them. For instance, when a student lends a pencil to another student that behavior could be reinforced. Perhaps a student tried to hang up his coat but it fell off the hook, and another student hung it up. That would be an act of kindness that could be reinforced. For example, Jeremy was a very self-centered fifth grader. He never noticed what any other student needed or had any idea of helping anyone else. Mrs. Morgan (Carolyn) wanted to help Jeremy become more kind to fellow students. She began praising other students for doing things that were kind. Over time she found dozens of small acts of kindness from many students. She made a point to describe the behaviors as she praised the students. The teacher expected it would take several weeks to catch Jeremy being kind. Nevertheless, she did notice him giving another student a sheet of paper. The teacher told Jeremy that she appreciated his helping a fellow student. Because she had praised him for giving another student a sheet of paper, she knew other instances of kind behavior would occur. The problem was for her to catch these examples before he gave up being kind to others. She found several more instances, and reinforced each behavior, and soon he was being more helpful to other students. The teacher had built the behaviors she wanted, but even more remarkably, other students started noticing acts of kindness and expressing their appreciation.

Sometimes people will overpraise an attribute and it backfires. Art once had a parent go overboard and tell her ten-year-old son he was the nicest boy in the world because of a little act of kindness. On his mother's birthday, the boy picked some spring flowers in the yard and put them in water for her. She found them on the table when she got home from work. This mother told her son he was the best boy in the world. Living up to her expectations was impossible so he destroyed the flowers. A thank you for being thoughtful would have strengthened the behavior and would have encouraged that and similar behaviors. Also, the disaster would have been avoided.

Chapter Review

Teachers must envision the behaviors necessary for each student to be a productive student-citizen. They must help them behave in ways that will lead to success. Art has had many teachers object by saying they have told their students how to behave thousands of times and it does not help. When teachers tell students what to do, they will usually change their behavior immediately and in doing so teach the teacher to direct their attention to problem behavior. Unfortunately, the attention probably strengthened the inappropriate behavior as well, and that behavior will occur more often in the future. If the new behavior does not result in need satisfaction, the inappropriate behavior has been strengthened while the appropriate behavior has been weakened. To maintain any behavior, it must be reinforced. The benefits of learning will not happen quickly enough to help young students learn the importance of working. The only primary reinforcer a teacher has control of is social approval. Teachers must learn to specify exactly how they want students to behave and to notice such behavior when they see it. A preschool teacher, Jana, the teacher in earlier examples, became a perfect example of specifying exactly how she wanted students to behave. She made it clear how students were to sit in their chairs and wait for papers and pencils. They were never to turn their paper over until she said it was time, and did not pick up their pencils until she finished the instructions. Everything she expected of students from the moment they arrived in class until they left was stated exactly. By reinforcing many instances of the specified behaviors, her students became highly disciplined. By the end of the year these students could manage their own behavior and all scored very high on the end-of-year evaluation.

Question and Answer

Question: I am a third grade teacher in the city where I grew up. My husband is a successful professional in our community. Both of my children are students in this district. I fear that if I adopt the strategies you recommend, I will become an outcast in my school. All of my colleagues and supervisors will conclude that I am doing everything wrong.

Answer: That is a good question. We have seen this happen. If you could get your principal or another teacher to see the benefits to students that you see, it would be easier. Have a few others read this book. We think you will find at least one other teacher to commit with you. Once you have one other teacher, and especially if you have your principal's blessing, you will have someone to share your success. However, do not try to push these ideas on others. We think that in six months other teachers will notice the difference with your students. Only then is it time gently to point out the reason. We wish you the best.

Effective Interactions Teachers Should Use and Why

What to Do	Rationale
Teachers should work at creating the appropriate behavior.	This is a necessary step to develop the cooperation that teachers must have to get students to work for the common good.
Teach every student to treat all others with respect.	Treating each other with respect is necessary for building a culture where each student works for the benefit of everyone.
Elementary teachers must develop a nurturing relationship with students.	Especially in primary grades, many students see themselves as needing help to succeed.
Teachers must use a powerful positive motivational process.	With an appropriate motivational process every student can be successful.
Teachers can use unlimited amounts of social approval.	Social approval is a primary reinforcer. No satiation effect is associated with social approval.
Social approval should be directed to all types of behavior. Praise correct answers, appropriate behavior, and behaviors that promote better learning.	Any behavior a teacher wants from students must be reinforced or the behavior will become less frequent.
Use differential social attention; it is the essential skill. The correct answers, appropriate behavior, and behaviors that promote learning should get the teacher's attention. Nonproductive behaviors do not get the teacher's attention.	This skill maximizes the reinforcers for appropriate behavior while reducing the chance of reinforcing inappropriate behavior. Given that such a small percent of students' responses can receive teacher attention, this is the only viable solution.
Reinforce simple behaviors immediately following the response.	Delayed reinforcers are nearly useless in developing behavior.
Reinforce continuation behaviors while the behavior is occurring.	If a continuation behavior is reinforced after a student stops, the student will only start working so he can stop. ☞

What to Do	Rationale
Specific praise is more effective than general praise.	Students need to know what they did to warrant the teacher's approval.
Distribute praise equally to all students. Some students can be praised for continuing to work while another is reinforced for remembering how to write effective sentences.	If only some students are getting the teacher's approval, other students will resent the teacher and those students who are getting her attention. They will disrupt the learning process. When this happens, students will not unite for a common purpose.
Distribute praise equally through-out the day.	Students will soon learn to work when they know they are going to be recognized. Eventually they will learn to work because that is the way to achieve. However, that will take at least much of a school year and maybe a few years.
When occupied with reading a story or helping some students, remember to occasionally look up and praise other students who are continuing to work.	If teachers omit this part of the method, inappropriate behavior will increase when the teacher is occupied with another activity.
Develop effective relationships with all students.	Students will experience less anxiety and learn more. Also, strong relationships will make the teacher's approval more powerful.

Interactions Teachers Should Avoid Using and Why

Interactions to Avoid	Rationale
Very rarely use tangible reinforcers.	Tangible reinforcers frequently create resentment among students.
Do not fall into the trap of only praising the best students.	All students need to learn to work. For the students who do not get equal recognition significant behavior problems will develop.

5

Building Successful Groups

A N ESSENTIAL ELEMENT OF TEACHING is first to get appropriate conduct and learning-related behaviors to occur. Only then can teachers strengthen those behaviors with the use of social approval. This chapter will focus on developing appropriate behavior.

Cari was preparing to meet her new class of 24 kindergarten students. She had been through this many times. She knew exactly what she was going to do and how to do it, although one thing was occupying her mind. Teachers had begun preparing for the new school year a few days earlier and she was thinking about a conversation with her new aide. It suggested the aide might find it difficult to accept the teaching process they would be using.

The aide, Kathy Raymond, had commented about how the class she worked with last year had been rowdy, defiant, and disrespectful and then said, "I see you don't have a stoplight for behavior problems. I would be happy to make one for you."

(For those readers not familiar with a stoplight system, it is a chart with large red, yellow, and green circles. There are clothes pins with the name of every student, and at the beginning of the day the pins for all students are clustered around green. The system is designed for teachers to warn and eventually punish students when their behavior is becoming disruptive.)

"We won't use a stoplight system," Cari responded.

Kathy said, "I'm sure you have your own system for discipline, just tell me what kind of chart you need."

"I don't have a discipline policy. Instead I have an appropriate behavior policy," Mrs. Williams answered.

"You are new here," Kathy replied. "Maybe you don't know the kids from this school. Believe me. You will need a discipline policy."

"No," Cari said, "we will teach children how we want them to behave."

"Good luck with that."

Cari replied, "I have many things I want put up on the walls, let's start by getting everything I use."

"Okay," Kathy said. "But just so you know, the teacher I worked for last year wouldn't have lasted five minutes without a stoplight system."

Cari replied, "I will find plenty of things for you to do, but you will need to learn to follow my lead in developing excellent behavior." Kathy rolled her eyes and walked away. Cari did not address the situation any further. However, two days later she was wondering if this would develop into a problem.

When Kathy arrived, Cari cheerfully greeted her and asked how many students were at the door.

Kathy answered, "Only a few now."

They worked together to finish the room. In a few minutes Cari went to the door. She had met the parents and most of the students in the last few days. However, she wanted the last five minutes before the bell to talk with parents and students. This gave her a chance to get to know more names and put names and faces together. She spoke briefly to every adult who brought a child. She also spoke to every child and called several students by name. The bell rang.

Cari said, "Boys and girls, listen for a minute. When we walk in line, we are orderly, we keep our hands to ourselves, and leave room between ourselves and the person in front of us. Follow me. Logan has his hands to his side, good job young man. Marla is walking nicely. Angel is leaving space so he doesn't crowd Cindy."

Her instructions created successful behavior and social approval strengthened those behaviors. She continued, "Follow me over to the cubbies. Mrs. Raymond labeled your cubby with your name. You always put your backpacks in your cubby. We will help you find where your backpack goes." As students finished putting their backpacks away, Cari helped them find a place to sit.

When the students were seated, she introduced herself and Mrs. Raymond. She had each student introduce themselves. Several times during this process she would ask another student if they remembered the name of the child who had just told the class his name. At first, the student might fail to remember. However, a few of the students already knew each other. When they had finished, the students were beginning to listen to each other; therefore, students were already succeeding in using a critical skill. By this point, though, two girls had crawled under their table and were grinning in defiance.

Kathy asked, "Want me to get them out?"

The surprising answer from Cari was, "No. They will come out soon enough."

When all of the students had introduced themselves, she had them move to the calendar area. She sent one table at a time and reminded students how to walk in line. She praised students who remembered to push their chair to the table. Cari also praised all reasonable approximations of walking, pushing in chairs, and sitting in the calendar area. However, if the students from one table forgot a step or two she would have the students from the table go back and practice. Cari never showed the slightest sign of frustration and the practice was not used as a consequence; instead, practice was a way to create success.

"We must learn to move around the classroom without bothering each other," she said. The two girls were still under the table. Nothing was said to them. All of the other students were in the calendar area.

Calendar time was very much like any other calendar activity for kindergarten students. When they finished calendar, the students remained seated in the same area. She had the students take turns telling something about themselves. Students told about their favorite game, food, or what they did over the summer. The two girls were still under the table; now, however, they were not grinning and were looking out to see when they would be noticed. Cari had specifically sat so that she could see if they did something that could not be ignored. In a few minutes, the girls came out from under the table and were looking at the group.

Cari invited the girls to join everyone else on the floor in the calendar area and room was made for them. Students were encouraged to ask each other questions. When students could use each other's names in the conversation, Cari mentioned it. After they had spent time getting to know each other, she had them return to their tables.

Kathy later asked, "Why didn't you let me get the girls out from under the table?"

Cari said, "Because they were not fulfilling any of their needs under the table they were bound to come out before too long. On the other hand, if we had attended to their behavior, they would have tried something new every day."

Kathy did not understand and shook her head as she walked away muttering something about never letting students get away with stuff like that. Readers should understand that neither the two girls nor the rest of the class was likely to miss the message. If they were like other humans, with a need to belong, they could not fulfill it while under the table. Cari would give her attention and admiration to those who were behaving in a way that would benefit the class's objective — to excel academically.

Many teachers would feel they had a responsibility to coerce the two girls to join the group; Cari, however, allowed them the autonomy to join the group when they were ready. If she had coerced the two girls out from under the table, she would have adversely affected most of the other students. If the girls had been climbing out the window, she would have responded differently.

While learning how to respond to inappropriate behavior is an important consideration, we suspect many teachers would also be afraid to ignore such behavior. They might fear another teacher or administrator would disapprove of their decision. We have wondered what it would be like to know the best way to handle the situation, but to fear widespread disapproval. Readers should further recognize the girls did not get away with anything, but instead missed getting equal recognition. If other students had stopped to think about it, they would say that they would rather be right where they were, not under a table.

Later in the morning, Cari started a conversation about how important it is for everyone to get along in a group. She asked them, "Do you like it when someone hits you?" They said no. She did not require every student to raise their hand to talk. She allowed an open discussion and used the opportunity to teach students not to interrupt each other. Because no one in the class liked getting hit by others, she suggested they make a rule that everyone would keep their hands and feet to themselves. Cari wrote the rule on the board and asked if anyone could read what had been written. No one could, but two of the students could read a few words. This gave her the opportunity to discuss how important it is to learn to read.

One student answered, "We know because we can trust you. You are a teacher." That answer presented a slight dilemma. She could not suggest that he not trust her, but she had to convince the students that they needed to learn to read.

Nevertheless, the class agreed that unless they learned to read they would have no way to know if she had written what they had decided. The discussion also focused on trust and how important it is never to lose the trust of those around you.

Next she asked them if they liked falling down and getting hurt. They all concluded they did not want to fall down unless they were playing. This became the reason for walking in the classroom and hallways. Then she asked the students, "When you are walking do you like it when the person behind you crowds into you?" The students agreed they did not like being crowded and agreed to a rule that students should leave space between themselves and the person in front of them. Cari followed up by saying, "Boys and girls, now we are going to practice walking to the door and lining up and then we will walk back to our seats. Students at this table can get up and walk to the door. That's the way to walk Bobbi, thank you. Adam is keeping his hands to himself, good job. Troy is remembering to leave space." She did this with the students from each table. As the students gathered near the door, she told them how to line up and praised those who followed her instructions. Once she got the students lined up at the door, she had them practice walking back to their seats. The students did well enough the first time so she did not have them practice again. She did not give any attention to those who crowded the student in front of them. All her attention was differentially directed to those who followed the rules. One boy said, "Mrs. Williams, she crowded me." Her answer was, "Everyone is learning. It will just take a few days." She continued, "Boys and girls, remember you can help teach your friends how to walk in line or you can show them how. We are here to help each other learn."

Teachers may want to think for a moment about everything the students learned during this lesson. They learned to listen in a group situation, which is different from listening to an adult who is talking directly to them. The students had to listen to answer her questions, and they wanted to show how well they had listened. The students learned to follow instructions because compliance got teacher recognition. From teacher recognition students developed a little more confidence that they could succeed in school. Students learned that the teacher would listen to what they had to say. These kindergarten students learned that their teacher would not get mad or punish a student for making a mistake and, yes, they learned to walk in line.

Cari continued for the next 30 minutes establishing the rules and expectations for more situations. She wrote the rules on the board and because kindergarten students are non-readers, she made little pictures beside the rules to help them remember. A few minutes later, she noticed it was time for recess. This was a perfect time to have the boys and girls practice walking to the door, lining up, and then walking in line on the sidewalk to the playground. She praised students for using "walking feet," keeping their hands to themselves, and leaving an arm's length of room between themselves and the person in front of them. After recess she again had the students line up and walk properly to their classroom door. When they got to their classroom, she started teaching the students how to recognize their classroom. Then they walked in and sat at their assigned table. She talked to the boys and girls about how they had done following the rules. The students had all done well with only a few exceptions. While she did describe the rules that students had disobeyed, Cari did not mention any students by name. This was the first day and it was dedicated to creating success and reinforcing that success. Even on this first day of school she had a good start on developing compliance and generating disciplined behavior. If major issues had come up, she would have reviewed the rules and had the students practice. If she had needed to correct a student, she would have done so without any consequences or shaming the student. Every teacher will have different rules; therefore we will not suggest what rules to have. The point is to help students learn and follow the rules for any classroom. Usually, older students will learn to follow the rules with little or no practice.

A point worth making is that compliance is an antecedent of co-operation. However, the issue confuses many professionals, and some call specific instructions "alpha commands." They advise teachers that a student can never be allowed to get away with noncompliance to direct instructions or alpha commands. However, this requires careful consideration, because the process of forcing the issue has serious consequences to both the individual and other students. The point those professionals are making is that any disobedience would show disrespect and undermine the teacher's authority. Readers by this point may understand that our process is not directed at stopping disobedience, but at building cooperation. A teacher who stops disobedience will have to stop many similar behaviors several times per day. However, a teacher who develops cooperative behavior will only need to reinforce a few instances of cooperation per week.

Because our main objective is to develop students who can excel personally and academically in school, we alert teachers to the consequences of shaming a student in front of his peers. We cannot disregard issues that could damage a teacher's relationship with students or the respect students show for each other. The objective in a classroom is to get students, acting autonomously, to cooperate with the teacher and each other 100 percent of the time; therefore, the concept of alpha commands is contraindicated. The development of cooperation begins with simple instructions to individual students and to groups of students. Most students will comply and every student gets to see other students do so, and consequently earn the teacher's approval. When a teacher is rarely coercive, all students will soon want her approval. Because some students are reinforced for following instructions, the entire group will learn. Nevertheless, the issue of noncompliance is a huge problem for many teachers. The problem of perfect compliance can be solved for the rest of the school year without treating it as an alpha problem. In just two or three weeks, a teacher can develop both compliance and complete cooperation. In those rare instances where she needs complete and instant compliance to a command, all students will comply without delay. They will understand the urgency and cooperate with the teacher.

After reviewing the students' success, Cari assembled them on the carpet to read a story. This provided a perfect opportunity to practice sitting and listening. She talked about the importance of staying seated during story time and asked if anyone knew why it was important. None of the students had a very good idea. However, some students thought it would hurt other students and another said, "It is against the rules."

Cari explained that while it could be disruptive to others, the most important reason to pay attention was that students must pay attention to learn. She continued, "You each need to pay careful attention so you can learn as much as you can." Cari also reviewed the rule about students keeping their hands to themselves. As she read the story, she praised students for remaining seated and keeping their hands to themselves. She asked lots of questions regarding the story and made sure many students got a chance to give the correct answer. However, many questions did not have a correct answer, but were asked to get an opinion from students.

Nearly everything she had done thus far was to get the students to think about what was important for learning. She wanted them to understand that each student had to contribute to the group's success, and the group depended on all students treating their classmates with respect. Cari recognized and appreciated those who treated others with respect, but students were not admonished for their shortcomings. She used differential social approval and avoided coercive interventions while helping students understand the importance of mutual respect in a classroom. Some students might learn to be perfectly respectful and cooperative during the first few days of school; however, if other students required more time that was okay. Because some students always behaved as expected, she had no reason to point out mistakes.

Readers might wonder at this point about the two girls who had crawled under the table. They were being treated just like every other student; Cari did not hold a grudge. As is often the case in Title 1 schools, there was an observer in the classroom that day. He noticed that after they rejoined the group, the girls were testing Cari a bit more than the other students. However, their behavior was not much out of line for kindergarten students. Cari apparently never noticed that the girls were still trying to disrupt the class. However, in talking to Cari later, the observer learned that she had noticed everything. She was not trying to eliminate inappropriate behavior; instead, she was working at establishing appropriate behavior. We want teachers to understand that eliminating inappropriate behavior is not the goal, because students do not actually eliminate behaviors. Students do not forget how to misbehave, they only inhibit certain behaviors in given settings. The imperative issue is to get the students voluntarily to inhibit inappropriate behavior and willingly to adopt cooperative behavior. Cari knew that in time all students would exercise their autonomy and become cooperative. She would never engage students in a battle of wills, because nothing good would come from such a battle. Furthermore, she knew she would have very few instances of defiance, because students in her class could not satisfy any psychological needs by becoming defiant.

At one point a student said something quietly to the girl next to her and the second girl responded in a loud voice. Cari did not scold the girl or mention any consequences, but instead started a conversation regarding talking too loud in a classroom.

Cari asked, "Do you think we should have a rule about talking too loud?"

Bobbi expressed her opinion, "Sometimes talking loud is okay. I was in a preschool play and I was supposed to talk loud."

Troy said, "Playing would be hard if we couldn't talk loud."

Cari listened carefully to everything the students had to say, then she suggested a rule for using inside voices whenever you are inside. She added, "But there will be exceptions."

Another student remembered when he was in Head Start they had a rule like that. The students agreed that they should have a rule requiring inside voices.

Jayson asked, "What happens to us if we forget?"

Cari answered, "It is my job to help students remember the rules and to obey them."

Jayson asked again, "But I want to know what is going to happen if I forget."

Mrs. Williams explained, "If you forget, I will help you remember. I don't think punishment would help you remember. You will learn soon enough."

Jayson proved his persistence, "When I am bad at home I get my butt smacked. Is that what happens here?"

Cari could not hold back a slight smile and added, "No one is going to get spanked. You will all make mistakes and forget a rule sometime. I will help you remember."

When the observer glanced at Kathy, he thought he could detect a look that reflected an attitude. Perhaps she was thinking, "I told you so."

Cari however, responded in a very different way. She said, "I will show you what I mean." She immediately started praising students for remaining seated, keeping their hands to themselves, and for participating in a respectful conversation. After praising about 15 students she stopped and asked, "Can you remember how to act for the next ten minutes?" Several students said in unison, "Yes." Two of the students almost shouted their answer.

Cari smiled and said, "When you are really excited about something that is a good time to show your feelings and talk a little bit loud."

The rest of the first day went much like the first part of the day. Cari had the boys and girls talk about behavior, rules, and the reasons for the rules. She would stop discussions and have the students practice following the rules. They practiced lining up, walking, finding their cubbies, keeping their hands to themselves, using inside voices, and not talking too loud. By the end of the day, the observer guessed that he had heard her recognize appropriate behavior more than a thousand times. This was the first day of kindergarten and most of the students had never been in school before. It was no surprise that there had been many examples of inappropriate behavior; however, by the end of the day the observer had trouble remembering which students had made mistakes. Everything he had seen that had gone right dominated his thoughts. He could not help but think the students were also remembering the right way to behave.

Cari had used some mistakes to establish and explain the rationales for the rules. In other cases, her response was simply to say, "I think we need to practice." She never said this in a way that suggested she was frustrated. She was not trying to find an alternate form of punishment. She was not trying to punish the group for the misbehavior of one or two students. The impression was more like she had little interest in which students had misbehaved. If two students did not walk in line appropriately, she did not interpret it as the students having done something wrong, but instead as implying that everyone, or at least many students, needed more practice. If the boys and girls could not remember how to make the letter *a*, it implied a need for more practice. If some students could not learn to leave room between themselves and the student in front of them, more practice was needed.

By the second day, and continuing through the first three weeks, Cari gradually introduced more assignments including counting and seatwork activities. The importance of staying in their seats and working quietly was reviewed. Students learned that when she was talking, they needed to remain quiet. However, teachers may want to note, Cari never uses the statement, "Bubble in your mouth." She simply taught them to be quiet when she or another student was talking. She described the proper behavior in every setting. They learned to remember how they should behave and why appropriate behavior was important. Students practiced until they had done everything right several times. She reinforced many instances of appropriate behavior for every student. Cari did not coerce students to behave appropriately. Instead, she remained alert for any student behaving appropriately and strengthened that behavior. No teacher can specify everything students should do, so while the message was sometimes never stated, the appropriate behavior got her approval. In those first few days, the most important task was to help the students remember how to behave. Reinforcers get students to remember the expectation; coercion and disapproval elicit shame or fear of being shamed.

Soon, the aide learned how to manage some activities. This allowed Cari to occasionally stay back and work with one or two students on lessons or issues that required practice. In just three weeks, students were choosing to behave according to the rules. A typical day would go very smoothly. The kindergarten students would enter the classroom following the opening bell and make their way to the cubby area where they took anything out of their backpacks they needed. After hanging up their backpacks they walked quietly to their seats without becoming distracted. After taking their seats they waited quietly, or talked quietly with others at their table. Most days only a few instances of disruptive behavior occurred. For instance a student might talk too loud, drop his backpack in front of his cubby, talk when he should be listening, or dump a box of crayons on the floor. These minor issues were never handled as misbehavior, but as certain students being unable to discipline their own behavior. This meant they needed to be praised more often for appropriate behavior. A typical response would be to increase the social approval for appropriate behavior. However, Cari would occasionally send a student back to fix the problem or to ask other students to help a particular student remember how to behave. When a student had to correct something he had done wrong, she always remembered to praise him for correcting his behavior. A student failing to behave appropriately always means he needs more praise for behaving appropriately. In that same three weeks, problem behavior was greatly reduced.

Perhaps the most important development of all was that the students were quickly learning to promote the common purpose. The students had become concerned about each other and wanted everyone to be successful. They addressed each other by name and the mutual respect they had for each other was evident. Cari no longer had to manage their behavior; they were, at least for the most part, managing it themselves. She had not used a discipline policy, but instead had used an appropriate behavior program.

During the next several months, if student behavior was slipping, she would revisit the practice procedure and increase the praise for conduct behavior. Following a school break, behavior problems would sometimes increase. This is typical, especially in the primary grades. In most of these instances, a renewed effort to praise more appropriate behavior for a few days was sufficient to reestablish students in managing their own behavior. Nevertheless, if student behavior became more of a problem, she would not hesitate to continue to focus on appropriate behavior. Students will not excel academically until they can manage their own behavior.

Many educators would likely consider so much practice of how students were expected to behave in various situations to be a terrible waste of time. However, that is not so. During the first four weeks of a school year, Cari seldom uses more than a total of ten hours to practice appropriate behavior. If a teacher uses those first few weeks correctly, the misbehavior in her classroom can be reduced by more than 90 percent. Many teachers spend 250 or more hours per year dealing with inappropriate behavior. By using the first three weeks correctly, Mrs. Williams greatly reduces the time required on discipline issues for the remainder of the year. The behavioral problems a teacher will encounter are not dependent on the students assigned to the class, but instead relate to the methods she uses to develop appropriate behavior.

For many teachers this does not strike a chord of truth. Because the same students are the problem day after day, year after year, and with almost every teacher, the conclusion that the students are the problem seems obvious. However, in this country, teachers consistently respond to problem behavior with similar intervention procedures; therefore, many students respond with similar and consistent misbehavior. The problem is nearly universal, because the problematic interventions are equally common.

Readers should also note that, given the methods we describe, students will have hundreds of additional hours to spend on academics. That is a huge difference. If even 20 percent of students can free up 25 percent more time for academic accomplishments, teachers would see a significant increase in academic scores. Inappropriate behavior in classrooms affects academic learning. However, as described in previous chapters, the stress associated with negative consequences also hinders academic performance. The most efficient way to produce a positive change in the academic performance of most elementary classrooms is to use an appropriate behavior program. However, assuming teachers want their students to excel academically, other changes will be necessary. Continue reading and the entire program will become clear.

As important as the emphasis on appropriate behavior is, an even more important difference from conventional practice is evident in Cari's classroom those first three weeks —students learn to manage their own behavior according to rules. They learn to take responsibility for their own behavior because doing so results in their satisfying their needs. Besides everything else they learn, each student learns that what is best for them is also best for everyone. Every student is working for the common good; consequently, their academic performance will improve.

Regarding Kathy's development, one example is worth discussing. Early in the school year, the principal came to Cari's classroom. She brought a new student who had just been enrolled that morning. The principal wanted to talk to Cari for a couple of minutes, so Kathy was left with the class. As Cari talked to the principal just outside the door, Kathy showed Eli his cubby and told him where to sit. She stepped in to finish the seatwork activity, and noticed Eli was not in his seat. Then she noticed he had moved his chair and was sitting on the floor.

She said in a cross voice, "Eli, sit in your chair, I won't have that kind of foolishness."

He slowly got up pulled his chair to the table and sat facing the other direction. Kathy went over and turned his chair around and pushed him up to the table. She said, "If you can't sit at the table you'll find yourself sitting in the corner."

He remained at the table and Cari came back into the room. She did not find out what had happened until the following day. When she had turned her back to help another student with a computer, Eli immediately stood up and turned his chair with the back against the table. He sat astraddle the chair facing the table. Cari heard Kathy say, "Eli, turn your chair around that is not the way we sit in a chair." He complied.

Later, on Eli's second day, Cari talked with Kathy about the issue. She explained why Eli was continuing his defiance. Kathy did not like hearing that the problem was considered her fault. "He's the problem," she said. "We have to do something to correct his behavior."

His behavior, including being out of his seat, distracting other students, and standing on his chair, continued for a few more days, but mostly when Cari was occupied with other students. However, by the next week Eli's behavior escalated, and within two days he was tipping over chairs, running through the room, and messing up papers on the desk. Kathy was constantly saying something to him when he misbehaved. Once she said to Cari, "We need consequences, because he will never learn if he doesn't lose some privileges."

Cari told her, "We will do something, but we will do it my way. You will not interfere. You will not talk to him when he is misbehaving." Then she set out the plan. "We will greatly increase the praises for appropriate behavior. These praises will be spread about equally throughout the class and he will get much praise whenever he is in his seat or following instructions. You need to watch."

Two seconds later Cari turned on the praise; besides her teaching she was praising students about four or five times a minute. This rate continued all day. A visitor commented that she had never heard anything like it —it sounded a little like a radio broadcast of a basketball game. Cari was constantly describing appropriate behavior. She kept this up for three days; however, on the third day Eli's behavior was nearly perfect. On the fourth day, Cari slowed the pace to more of a normal rate of praise for that early in the school year. Eli's behavior continued to be good for several days with only a few minor problems that were normal for kindergarten students. During this period Cari had to keep an eye on Kathy. Once, when Eli was behaving inappropriately, she had to stop Kathy from scolding him.

Readers should understand that Eli was not hurting anyone else, and was not endangering himself. During this time he had lost valuable work time, but any other course of action would have made it worse. If Cari had not been working hard on the issue herself, we would expect the problem to spread to other students. Even Kathy understood that the previous year this would have become an issue that went beyond the misbehavior of one student. To her credit, she worked hard to control her instinct to intervene. The behavior problem disappeared and Eli reached his academic goals by the end of the school year.

Before the end of the first semester, Kathy had learned to manage student behavior and many learning activities. She could take the students to recess or lunch without any help from Cari. In most situations students behaved very well for her. Their behavior did not slip much when she supervised the students. In those instances when student behavior did slip a little, Kathy could adjust and they would behave appropriately. Before the end of the first semester, Kathy expressed what she had learned. She said, "I must admit your way of teaching students to behave appropriately is much better. I would never have believed it, but punishment is almost never necessary."

Cari replied, "I'm glad you accepted my way. You are a big help with the students."

Kathy asked, "Why don't all teachers do it this way?"

"I wish I knew. Schools would run better and students would learn more if most teachers used a positive approach to teaching."

Kathy replied, "Sometimes I tell other teachers they should adopt a good behavior policy."

Cari smiled and nodded her agreement.

Applying the methods in any primary grade classroom would be very similar to the kindergarten classroom, but a few differences might be evident. Establishing rules would be much the same, although even first and second graders will be able to contribute more to the rules and rationales. Second graders would also learn and remember rules a little more quickly than kindergarten students. A second grade teacher should assume that it would take nearly as much praise to establish excellent behavior. One difference would be that second graders should require less behavioral practice. Where Cari had the students practice following each rule several times, less practice would be needed with primary grade students. However, in the end it is not what is expected of the students, but their behavior that determines how a teacher will proceed. We would assume second and third graders would learn a little more quickly from the praise directed toward other students. As early as the second grade, the influence of the interactive process happens sooner. Second grade teachers can probably spend a little more time discussing and helping students understand how they can help each other. We would want the common purpose of the class to show.

Following is an example that did not go so well and an explanation of how it could have been handled. Molli Bronson, a second grade teacher, was known for never giving in to students' irresponsible behavior. Jaylynn, a seven-year-old girl, who had recently been through several foster homes, was new to the school. The school had free breakfasts available for all students. However, on this third day of the school year, Jaylynn had chosen to play instead of going to breakfast. When she went into class, she told Mrs. Bronson she was hungry. Molli's response was, "That is your fault. You can't have anything now." (School policy would have allowed her to get something from the cafeteria that could be taken to class.)

This consequence was supposed to teach Jaylynn never to choose play instead of breakfast. Instead, it resulted in her refusing to participate and causing considerable trouble all morning. By 11:00 Molli was asking another teacher for help. She said, "If she can't behave responsibly, she can just get out."

The school subsequently moved the girl to a class for students with behavioral issues. Molli clearly thought that was exactly where she belonged. Some teachers want to get difficult students out of their classrooms, because they are concerned that such students will hurt the class's academic results for the school year. Molli could have adopted procedures that would have helped this student in a regular classroom. Jaylynn was very intelligent and could have contributed to the academic progress of the group. The teacher's strict response would also most likely interfere with the performance of many students. Breakfast cannot be denied to a second grader on the third day of school without damaging the trust most of the class has in their teacher. We also want to point out that a diversity of students, with different strengths, weaknesses, and problems, is a big advantage to a teacher. When a teacher directs her attention to appropriate behavior while inappropriate behavior is occurring, the power of the culture is strengthened. Every student becomes more committed to controlling his own behavior.

Administrators often advise teachers never to attend to inappropriate behavior, which is usually considered sound advice. We also advocate withholding attention to inappropriate behavior as part of the differential social attention process. Nevertheless, we also advise teachers to use good judgment about being nurturing and treating students with humanity. We concur that teaching students to get their breakfast before class time is important. However, teachers need to understand that consequences are not likely to be effective. Perhaps the teacher should think about what she, as a parent, would do if her daughter had gotten up too late to sit and eat breakfast. Most parents would find something for their daughter to eat in the car, and plan to continue working at teaching her to get up on time. This second grade girl needed to know that she mattered as a person. Tender loving care will accomplish more than harsh consequences. If the teacher were worried about other students deciding they too could wait and eat breakfast in class, teaching them to eat breakfast before school is easy. By asking for a show of hands of the students who had remembered to eat breakfast, she could express her appreciation to those who were concerned about helping to preserve class time. Also, getting the student something she could eat in class would result in her behaving appropriately for several minutes. That would be sufficient for the teacher to use positive skills to parlay those minutes into hours of good behavior. The teacher would want to review with all students the importance of remembering to eat breakfast before coming to class. She could, for a few days, get a show of hands of all the students who had eaten breakfast before class, and express her appreciation to those students. If for some unlikely reason, the problem continued with a few students, the issue could be easily resolved. A simple adjustment of having a teacher or aide occasionally walk through the cafeteria a few times per week and pleasantly interact with their students for remembering to eat breakfast would guarantee effective results in a week or two.

Teachers sometimes face another issue they must solve. Some groups of students will be hyperactive or fidgety. Teachers get the feeling that in some groups the constant motion is contagious. Of course, such behavior is not literally contagious; however, because anything that affects one student will affect all students, the constant movement of several students can affect the entire class. We have seen this more often in the primary grades, but all teachers may encounter the problem.

Everything we have described still holds true. Students can keep much of their hyperactive behavior in check if the teacher is accomplished in using differential social attention. If a positive motivational system, using a primary reinforcer, is in place, students will suppress hyperactive behavior, at least to a point. Nevertheless, teachers will encounter situations where students cannot continue working as the teacher would like.

We will describe an example from a kindergarten class of 20 students. Several students were hyperactive. The teacher, Shae Lynn Daniels, was superior in her ability to motivate students to inhibit the need to move. However, one year in particular she had a class that had more trouble controlling their need to move. Despite Shae Lynn's skills, nearly every day she would encounter instances where most of the students would reach a point where almost none of them could concentrate any longer. The solution, that might seem counterintuitive, is to give students more breaks than would usually be necessary.

We have, however, seen instances where school principals had trouble tolerating this solution. In the example that Art is most familiar with, the teacher would work especially hard to maintain students' concentration. However, she also kept a close eye on how effective the reinforcers were at maintaining the work-related behaviors. When several students were unable to concentrate any longer, she would suspend all academic work. Students would gather in an open area and she would encourage them to dance. The dancing would continue for several minutes before she would have them resume their academic work. At times, especially in the winter, the breaks could be given once or twice a day and perhaps a few days a week. Teachers will immediately understand that so many extra breaks take a significant chunk out of curriculum time. This teacher had, for several years, proved her ability to get the most out of students. Because this teacher's classes always scored very high on end-of-year evaluations, Art trusted her to do what was best for her students. The year in question was no different. Despite what many educators think, plenty of time is available in a school year for all students to learn everything required to reach grade level standards. This teacher's expectation was to ensure the success of the students and she recognized what was necessary to accomplish success with that class.

Differences in Upper Grades

These methods are applied much the same way from kindergarten through third grade. Minor differences as mentioned above are easy adjustments for teachers. By the upper grades some differences will become obvious. However, our experience has been that teachers with a year or two of experience in the upper grades do not have trouble with these differences. Most upper grade teachers quickly understand the minor adjustments that must be made in applying the process with older students.

Some differences involve the rules and rationales for the rules. Older students will have a good understanding of what rules are needed and why. Students can still make suggestions, but discussions will not be lengthy. Obviously, the students can write the rules and make charts to remind themselves of the rules.

Gradually, from kindergarten on, teachers will spend more time teaching students to solve conflicts for themselves. Consequently, conflict resolution should take less of their time. As students become older, teachers must be more willing to let them solve problems for themselves. Teachers should understand this is an ongoing process. Even kindergarten teachers need to teach conflict resolution. However, as students get older they spend more time beyond the supervision of teachers. They must develop conflict resolution skills or everything accomplished in the elementary school can be for naught.

Another issue becomes important as students get older. They must have a value system and act on those values. Because learning to behave according to one's values is an extension of rule-ordered behavior, the process begins by the age of four. Many teachers may worry that sufficient time is not available for teaching social development. When students become powerful learners, more than enough time can be found to develop value-ordered behavior.

Teachers will still have to deal with misbehavior. Upper grade teachers will find it necessary to address behavior that is disrespectful of others or disruptive to the functioning of the group; nevertheless, the same principles apply. Punishment and consequences will still impede efforts to establish a functional group. In fact, such procedures might be even more damaging to classroom objectives in the upper grades.

The rules will still be the rules and it will take social approval to help students follow them. Many behaviors that kindergarten teachers deal with will still be evident through the upper grades. Teachers can sometimes find this very frustrating. Many upper grade teachers do not like dealing with pushing, shoving, hitting, gossiping, disrespect, and lack of concern for education. However, many elementary teachers will find themselves needing to deal with such issues. For example, if Jeannie, a fourth grader runs to be first in line for lunch, the teacher may have a few ways to respond. The harsher the consequence, the more likely the problem will become worse. Many teachers would immediately send the girl back to walk and take a position at the end of the line. That consequence is logical and if handled calmly might work. However, the possibility exists that it might not have the desired effect. (Although teachers should note that the same possibility exists for other procedures.) Teachers must be aware of whether their procedures are working. The issue with using a consequence is that words from the teacher provide immediate attention for the undesired behavior. The possibility exists that despite the consequence, the attention may serve to increase the frequency of running to get in line. While the student will almost undoubtedly comply with the teacher's instructions, it does not mean the consequence will be effective. Even if the behavior does decrease for several days, the teacher must find ways to strengthen the appropriate behavior. Effectiveness can only be determined by noticing if the instances of students running to get in line becomes less frequent and subsequently more appropriate behavior is evident. However, another problem with using consequences for inappropriate behavior is that sometimes, while the exact behavior decreases, other disruptive behaviors will increase. A student may quit running to get in line, but continue her defiance by being out of her seat.

Another teacher we know provided us with a slight twist on handling the situation of a boy running to lunch. Carolyn Snider said nothing to the third grade boy (Dustin) while he was running to get in line. However, she praised several students for walking in line and being respectful of their classmates. When the line arrived at the lunch room, they stopped as they were always expected to do. She chose several students who had maintained orderly behavior from the classroom to the cafeteria and allowed them to go to the front of the line. Dustin was the last to go into lunch. Those students who had maintained self-discipline and walked in an orderly way through the halls got the privilege of being first into the cafeteria. When Dustin walked past, Carolyn bent over and quietly said, "Remember to walk all the way to lunch. I will notice so you can be first in line sometimes." By handling the problem in this way, she did not give attention to inappropriate behavior while the student was misbehaving. However, she must remember to notice when Dustin walks through the halls.

She might find it useful to review the rules before going to lunch the following day. With this process, Carolyn can be sure Dustin will walk appropriately for at least several seconds. She only needs a few seconds of the appropriate behavior to strengthen it. She can create success so the appropriate behavior can be reinforced. Remember the appropriate behavior can never be taught by responding to the inappropriate behavior. The only hope a teacher has to get the appropriate behavior to continue occurring is to create success and reinforce the behavior.

With older students, teachers may want to place more emphasis on students following instructions immediately. Although important for younger students, it becomes more critical for older students to respond immediately. Many people will become impatient with older students who put off responding. In many situations, teachers may want students to acknowledge instructions and follow them immediately. However, in the example we will use, an acknowledgment was not necessary.

Lynn Rexberg, a fourth grade teacher, said to her class, "Please put your library books away; we are going to do our journals now."

Hunter kept reading and did not put his book away. This would irritate many teachers. Lynn wanted to help Hunter learn to follow instructions, but she also knew that trying to exact consequences for his failure to respond would only compound the problem. To punish his noncompliance would also negatively effect his reading, which no teacher would want to do. Any positive or negative consequence affects all behaviors that occurred immediately before the consequence. The use of negative consequences would also prompt some type of negative emotional response. Attempting to repair a negative emotional response would require more work than dealing with the noncompliance. Instead, Lynn praised several students for their immediate compliance.

Initially the pointed praise technique did not appear to change Hunter's behavior. Lynn continued helping other students with their journals. She helped any student who needed assistance and expressed her approval to students who were working. In about three minutes, Hunter put his book away and got out his journal. Lynn made a mental note to talk to him later. Within a couple of minutes Hunter was working in his journal. He, too, was recognized for his work. Later that day she took Hunter aside and mentioned to him that he had continued reading. He said, "I wanted to finish the chapter."

She reminded him that she had given a three-minute notice and that students could stop reading at the most convenient time during that three minutes. Hunter protested, "I didn't hear you."

Arguing about whether he did or did not hear her would be pointless. She said, "Because of how important the first few minutes of a new lesson are, immediate compliance is necessary. Otherwise I would have several students who would not know what was expected during the next lesson."

She saw little reason to pursue the issue any further. He had eventually complied and other students were not disrupted. Lynn made a mental note that the next several times when Hunter immediately complied she would be sure to recognize his response. Furthermore, she would make a point to recognize several students for their immediate compliance and ensure that the issue would remain isolated. The issue is not whether Hunter got away with noncompliance; the issue is whether she can get all students in the future to be ready for the next lesson. Remember, consequences for inappropriate behavior cannot teach appropriate behavior. The appropriate behavior is taught by getting it to occur and reinforcing it.

One concern in the upper grades is that major misbehavior can be more difficult to handle. However, upper grade teachers should be aware of a major advantage they have — in the upper grades, most students will respond appropriately. Teachers can count on the expectations of peers to have a greater influence on how particular students respond. The trick is to get most of the class to behave appropriately and express their expectations of other members. By the upper grades, students have had more experience participating on teams and belonging to other types of groups. Teachers will find that instead of taking up time with practice, which would be resented by older students, building a well-functioning group is more important. Each student should take pride in how well they do academically and be committed to the success of other students. By spending more time on this, the teacher can enhance the power of the group in developing responsible behavior. This can become a major factor in reducing serious misbehavior. However, despite the methods a teacher uses, she will at some point encounter serious misbehavior. Nevertheless, the methods we have described will reduce the number of problems, the severity of inappropriate behavior, and increase the success in resolving issues. As compliance becomes cooperation, serious misbehavior becomes improbable. In Chapter Eight we discuss techniques for dealing with very serious behavior problems.

With older students, teachers can create a well-functioning class in just a few days; therefore, they can concentrate on the behaviors that promote learning and direct most of their reinforcers to academic accomplishments and the behaviors that resulted in those accomplishments. In the upper grades teachers will, most often, be more matter of fact in their praise statements. The statements will often imply social approval as opposed to explicitly stating it.

Doris Holmgren walked around her fifth grade classroom, commenting on the students' work. For instance, she said, "Mary is moving right along on her essay. Dontae is started. Roxanne has a neat paper. Students remember to develop your essay from the topic sentence." She stopped and said, "I am seeing some unique ideas on how to get more citizens to vote. Don't be afraid to write what you think." She did not direct much attention to students continuing to work because they usually worked like she expected. She was mostly providing recognition for ideas and quality of the students' work.

One of the biggest problems facing schools is that of students excluding other students from play or socialization. As students reach the upper grades they start deciding who they want as their friends. In the upper grades, when many students are beginning to restrict their friendships, unification of the class is even more important. The greater the academic and social diversity, the more important it is for the group to be unified and work for the benefit of each other. The same situation would exist for a team or a choir. However, coaches and choir directors have a major advantage, because the participants have much in common and the unified purpose is always clear; thus, group leaders find it easier to promote mutual respect.

Unfortunately, teachers find it more difficult to prevent students from excluding others, because it almost never happens when they are nearby. Both boys and girls will try to exclude certain students from their activities. Girls may just ignore a particular student. However, at least in the upper grades, boys will frequently be mean in excluding others. For instance, when they are playing basketball, they may specifically say to another student that he cannot play with them because he is not good enough. They may add that he is too slow or that the game is just for guys that were on a team the year before. Because exclusion can lead to bullying, the problem becomes even more important. The more degrading the exclusion, the greater the threat of serious retaliation.

We will describe an example from a sixth grade class. Roberta Bostic, a young teacher, stepped outside for a breath of fresh air just before the end of recess. She found Jason, a small, non-assertive but intelligent boy sitting outside the classroom door. At first she thought he might be sick or hurt, but that was not so. He was upset because the other boys would not let him play basketball with them. After a little prodding, he told her that the boys had said that he was not good enough to play. They had continued by saying he always lost the ball and did dumb things. He told her that he knew he was not as good as the others, but he wanted to learn.

She was not sure what to do about the issue, because if she addressed it directly, the others might treat him worse than ever. After school she talked to Donna Sister, the counselor, and decided that she would come in and lead a discussion about students being excluded.

At a predetermined time Donna walked into the sixth grade classroom. Roberta said to the class, "Some schools have had a problem with students being excluded by their classmates from activities. This frequently happens during recess or in the lunch room. The problem has been getting worse in some schools and we want to prevent it from getting worse at our school. Our counselor, Mrs. Sister, has been talking to classes about the problem. Today she came to talk to us."

Donna said, "Thank you, I am so happy to be here and I think I know most of you. Schools in this area have been having more instances of students excluding other students from activities. I'm sure some of you have seen this happen or maybe you have even been excluded. Can anyone tell me how it would feel to be left out of activities by class-mates?" She waited several seconds, but no one answered. She said, "I know it's hard, but we are just talking about how it might feel. You don't have to say that it happened to you or a friend."

After a few seconds, Rhonda spoke up. "It would make you feel bad. It would make you feel like no one liked you."

Donna said, "Yes I'm sure it would. I remember once when I was not invited to a birthday party, and I was hurt. Can anyone tell us more about how someone might feel?"

Janet spoke up and said, "I think I would be hurt and mad both."

Donna replied, "That's a good answer. I think a person might be upset with the people she thought were her friends."

Bert spoke up, "I had a friend at my last school who was always left out and he was so mad he wanted to hurt everybody."

Donna said, "Thank you for sharing that. I can see how that could happen. I don't think I know you as well as most of the other students. Are you Bert?"

"Yes."

"What is your last name Bert?" she asked.

"Lawton."

Donna made a quick note on her pad reminding herself to talk to Bert in private. She continued, asking for others to say how they might feel.

A few more hands went up. She called on Lana. Lana explained that she would feel awful and just want to go hide. Donna continued, "I think all of you would feel bad if you were the one left out. I have talked to several teachers about this issue. We really want to be sure that stu-dents in our school are all treated equally. What do you think we can do to prevent the problem at our school?"

Janet spoke up. "I think the students have to be the ones to stop it. We all need to remind each other and never let it happen."

Kara Lee added, "Janet is right, but it is hard sometimes."

Bert spoke up, "I didn't want my friend to be picked on, but I couldn't stop it."

Janet said, "I don't want Bert to get picked on because he stands up for a friend. But we cannot allow our friends to be discriminated against."

Donna said, "'Discrimination' is a good word. Excluding others because of race, religion, or gender is very serious. In fact, adults could get into legal trouble for discriminating against other people. However, other reasons would also be bad. It would not be right to exclude someone just because he doesn't know the names of all the great basketball players."

The discussion continued for several more minutes. Then Donna said, "How many of you think, we as a school, have a responsibility to be sure that no student is ever discriminated against?"

Rhonda and Janet raised their hands immediately. Bert hesitantly raised his. Other students soon raised their hands until every student's hand was in the air.

Donna said, "Wonderful, every hand is raised. That means you are all committed to being good citizens." She closed the discussion and said that teachers were going to be watching the playground carefully to see that all students were included. Mrs. Bostic said that she too would be keeping an eye on the problem. She also said that she would be reminding students before every recess and asking specifically after recess if anyone saw other students being excluded. While the problem can be addressed after it happens, teachers can help prevent the problem by insisting in the classroom that everyone be treated with respect.

In previous chapters we described how punishment and most consequences for inappropriate behavior invariably result in emotional responses that render the student and perhaps the entire class incapable of learning for a period. Because of this effect, which is even more evident in group situations, teachers must learn how to approach the development of appropriate behavior through positive methods. The essential message of this chapter is that effective methods always approach conduct behavior by developing the appropriate behavior. We have found that many teachers find it difficult to accept that all behavior problems in their classrooms are best addressed by teaching the appropriate behavior. However, excluding rare exceptions, the following methods will address the issues. Teachers should:

1. Describe appropriate behavior and the rationale for such behavior
2. Be sure that inappropriate behavior gets the least attention
3. Be sure that appropriate behavior is recognized and appreciated
4. Create opportunities for all students to be successful
5. Empower students to excel

Question and Answer

Question: I am a second grade teacher. I know my students. I could imagine most of my students doing something similar to crawling under a table. However, none of my students would have responded like the students in the example. Obviously, the students are different. Why do you think ignoring will work with all students?

Answer: We have on occasion seen similar situations where students did not respond as well as they did to Cari. Two differences from our example could account for what you are describing. One is what the students have already learned before they crawl under the table. The most important difference, though, usually depends on what the students learn while they're under the table. Think of students crawling under the table as undertaking an experiment. They want to see what the teacher will do. Once they have an answer to that question, they will know how to avoid expectations. Many teachers think students misbehave because they are bad. More often, they have embarked on learning something about the teacher. If they can find a way to control the classroom, they can be heroes with other students, and most expectations will get lost in the chaos. If they can turn the classrooms into fun and games, they can, although at their own expense, temporarily be the winners. Careful observation will reveal that the students are thoughtfully, but perhaps not obviously, watching the teacher. They are watching to see how often she will look at them. The students are assessing how concerned (or nervous) the teacher becomes about their behavior. They may be watching to see how other students will react to their being under the table.

A teacher's success at addressing the problem behavior will depend on several factors. First, if she just ignores the students under the table, the process will fail. Instead, she must use differential social attention. She must ensure that all other students would prefer to be participating in the teacher-directed activity. Her success, in part, depends on her faith that the process will work. In fact, a lack of confidence is almost certain to cause it to fail. If the teacher is concerned about what her colleagues or supervisors will think, her body language will reveal to the students that they can prevail. In our example, Cari positioned herself so she could notice if the girls did something she could not ignore; however, she was not watching them. Teachers should understand that students will join the group when they begin to wish they were participating in the class activities. The girls were not voluntary members of the class. However, they soon became voluntary participants in the culture they observed. Their change in attitude was because the teacher used differential social attention. The success of other students made the class activity more desirable than being isolated under a table.

A more difficult situation could exist if students have previously learned that such behavior always forces teachers into responding. This will be most difficult if the students have learned that this teacher will eventually attend to them. However, for the teacher it means she must be prepared to continue the process longer. Sometimes, students have learned from previous teachers that attention is soon forthcoming. In these instances, the teacher needs to make the lesson so reinforcing that the target students will not want to continue their defiance.

Effective Interactions Teachers Should Use and Why

Effective Interactions	Rationale
Especially early in the school year teachers need to use very high rates of social approval.	To establish appropriate behavior, teachers must reinforce such behavior. Social approval, because it is a primary reinforcer, is most effective.
The use of differential social attention is a very powerful tool in group settings.	Teachers see thousands of behaviors per day in their classes. They must find ways to maximize the effectiveness of their limited attention.
Have students practice the behavior they need to learn.	This practice does not have to be limited to academic material.
Teach all students to treat everyone with respect.	Despite teachers not wanting to deal with social issues, this is a major part of helping students excel. Also, the significant problem of bullying has made it impossible for teachers to disregard social issues any longer.
Compliance is important, but it cannot get in the way of education.	Too often teachers are so threatened by isolated instances of noncompliance that they make it their mission to demand absolute compliance. Teachers will get complete compliance soon enough.
To stop bullying, teachers should be sensitive to students.	Students are sometimes trying to tell their teacher something, without verbally explaining themselves. Teachers cannot read minds, but they can read expressions and they can also make it safe for students to express themselves.

Interactions Teachers Should Avoid Using and Why

Things Teachers Should Avoid Doing	Rationale
Teachers should not allow expectations from other teachers to prevent them from using methods that are effective.	What is best for students should motivate teachers.
The determination never to give in to irresponsible behavior can sometimes get in the way of teaching responsible behavior.	Too often teachers have learned isolated aspects of behavioral science to the exclusion of even more important principles, or how the human brain works. If teachers do not create success, they have failed.
Successful teaching is less about consequences and more about connections.	Humans learn best from those with whom they have strong connections.

6

Developing Effective Learners

INALLY we have come to perhaps the most important chapter in the book. All of the good conduct in the world does not make students smart. To build effective learners, teachers, at any grade level, must develop the behaviors necessary for learning. Many of those behaviors are the same for students from preschool through the college years.

Many years ago Art was visiting several public school classes in a university community. He visited schools in the poorest area of town and the best areas. One day in April he was in a middle-income area. Nearly all the students had scored between the 40th and 60th percentile on achievement tests. His appointment was to visit Martha Daniels' sixth grade class; when he arrived, they were working on a writing assignment. He sat in the back of the room and watched as the students worked independently. The teacher was moving around the room and stopping to read what some students had written. She seldom said anything to a student. After a few minutes she asked Art if he would like to move around the room and look at some papers. He said yes. She made an announcement to the class that he would also be coming around to see their work. Most of the students never looked up. The quality of the writing impressed him and he asked her opinion of the students' work. She said that she expected all of her students to score above the 90th percentile in all academic areas. He asked what their scores were at the beginning of the year. Martha responded, "The average was just over the 50th percentile." On subsequent visits he learned more about how she taught and some points in this chapter are similar to the methods she used many years ago. Art followed up at the end of the year and found the students had validated her prediction. The methods he had seen were worth remembering.

Martha constantly kept a primary issue in mind: students had to learn how to learn. Every student needs to develop the confidence to learn, gain the basic skills of learning, and learn to work independently. The conduct behavior of students is only part of the equation. They must also develop the academic behavior necessary for excelling in school. We describe the process for developing learners in this chapter.

Students needing the confidence to learn reminds us of a conversation Art recently had with a physician. The physician held that people, at any given moment, are in a state of either hunting or hiding. Humans, he continued, much prefer the physiological feelings associated with hunting and do not like the feelings that drive them into hiding. This idea is easy to understand when considering a caveman who was hunting for food or hiding from larger animals. However, the idea applies equally to a student who is in pursuit of knowledge or conversely hiding from the possibility of being identified as a failure. Teachers must first get students to come out of hiding, because they cannot learn if they are trying to avoid failure. In Chapter Two we described how captive primates respond to aversive stimuli. Unfortunately for teachers, a student who is in danger of being identified as a failure has other alternatives that were not available to captive primates. He may try to sink into his chair hoping to hide, or he can make it clear that he does not care. This strategy is frequently effective in getting a teacher to give up on the student. If a student does not care about what is taught, why would she care? Fortunately, teachers have access to methods to get students to care. Creating success and reinforcing that success always gets students to want to succeed.

Students can create a more difficult problem. They can create their own hunt. If they go in search of a way to disrupt the entire class, they can make school difficult for everyone. Presumably, they have no chance of driving the teacher into hiding, but they can turn the classroom into a game that the teacher can never win. Teachers must be equipped with techniques to help students become cooperative and enthusiastic learners.

Starting from the first moment, teachers will want to be sure that every student is successful. They can show students that they are not there to find mistakes or punish; they are there to help students succeed. While a positive relationship is a good start, it will not automatically create success. Teachers will need to master several interactive strategies. They should start the school year with simple lessons so that all students can be successful. A simple and basic technique is to ask questions and be sure that every student has a chance to answer correctly. When teachers ask questions, some students will get the answer correct. Using the process described earlier, once a student gets the answer correct, the teacher will ask the same question to many students. With this process she can assure that everyone will get the right answer and no one is identified as a failure. A teacher who does not criticize, but instead always finds a way to generate correct answers and recognizes those answers will keep all students involved in a hunt for success.

Teachers can make another mistake that will send students into hiding. Some students will have a terrible time at the beginning of the year and they may be behind in some areas for several weeks or even months. However a teacher cannot know after one day — or even 90 days — whether a student is failing. If he eventually succeeds, he was in the process of succeeding. By comparison, a baseball team that is six runs behind in the bottom of the ninth inning is not in the process of losing unless they eventually lose; however, they cannot win if they give up. We have seen students who were seriously behind in reading for several months catch up in just a few weeks. Remember the example of Dusty from Chapter Three. Unfortunately, schools usually have a policy, even for the primary grades, that teachers must identify any student who is failing. Parents are notified of the student's status. Every school Cari has taught in has had such a policy; therefore, she must guard against letting this affect how she treats the student. If a child is treated like he is going to fail, he will fail. Instead teachers must always approach students' lack of success from a different point of view. Art always advises teachers to develop a mindset that the student has not yet succeeded.

To be successful, teachers have to find ways to get all students actively to pursue learning. To accomplish this, they must simultaneously free students from a fear of failure and teach them how to learn. While we must choose an order of presentation, teachers will be working on all the skills associated with learning almost simultaneously. In the previous chapter, we saw Cari start by teaching kindergarten students to listen on the first day of school. Readers will recall that she asked students the name of the student who had just introduced himself. The intent was to help children actively listen to each other and develop communication skills. The students had to listen to know how to walk in line, sit in a circle, and show respect for each other. By requiring students to practice everything required of them, she was preparing them to learn.

Having students walk in line or hang up their backpacks was only part of what they were learning. These were easy lessons that everyone could learn, but the students had to listen, remember, and act on what they remembered. She had created a complex chain of behaviors and as soon as the students were successful in performing them, she reinforced their success. As a result, the complex chain was learned. All learning for the remainder of their lives depends on that mental process. The goal is to get students listening, remembering, and following instructions; these enhance self-confidence and become the foundations of academic success.

Because the basic objective is for every student to be successful, we advise teachers to start building success on the first day with easy expectations. We understand teachers are eager to get started and have a long list of matters to cover in the school year. Nevertheless, helping students realize that they have nothing to fear and can succeed is the first order of business.

Success even with the most simple of tasks will boost every student's confidence. In just days, most students can develop a more positive self-image and trust in the teacher to help them be successful. Students will understand the teacher is a leader dedicated to creating universal success. When students recognize their progress, every student's amygdala can fulfill its duties of assigning an emotional tag to cognitively processed information. When the prefrontal cortex is unimpeded, it can retrieve incredible amounts of information. The teacher who avoids creating psychological stress has taken the first step in transforming the students into capable learners. The transformation can happen in just a few weeks; students spend the rest of the year learning. By correctly preparing students, teachers will spend less time chasing problem behavior and more time helping students learn. In too many classrooms, this is not happening; nevertheless, the problem is the methods, not the teachers. Schools must give teachers methods that develop the brain activity necessary for learning.

Besides the efforts to develop appropriate conduct behavior, teachers must, from the first day on, teach academic lessons. Whether a teacher is conducting circle time, teaching calendar, giving a writing assignment, or reviewing concepts, she must create success and keep an emphasis on listening and remembering. She will ask many questions and get some students to answer correctly. When several students have given the correct answer, she moves to other questions, but never forgets to go back and ask the same questions that students answered correctly a few minutes or even a few days earlier. This process is designed to help students remember for longer periods. When this process is combined with social approval for remembering, information retrieval becomes easy. By using this process day after day, teachers will find students are soon remembering more information. Nevertheless, Art has seen many teachers become impatient with this process and discontinue it before all students could remember for considerable periods. Sometimes he has become impatient with teachers who would later argue that the students could not learn. If children can learn how to play a video game or use the remote, they can learn in school. This process may take longer with some students; however, teachers must continue until all students can remember.

Teachers should remind students often that correct answers are the result of listening and remembering. When students are daydreaming, they may be oblivious to the fact that learning is dependent on paying attention. Teachers must be careful about assuming students learned to listen the previous year. Until all students show the ability to listen and remember what was said, teachers must continue to work the two-part process of asking questions while reinforcing listening and correct answers.

Educators are sometimes surprised to learn that students adapt their behavior to every new teacher. Until students have been successful in school for several years, they will have some anxiety with every new teacher. We have seen many teachers devastated when they see their students, who did very well the year before, move onto next grade with a teacher who uses traditional methods. Frequently, traditional methods have a disastrous effect on students, even those who had excelled with a previous teacher. This reality sometimes leads to a criticism of our methods. The argument claims that if the methods were good, the students would be changed forever. That is an unrealistic expectation. If children could not adapt to a new situation, the human race would never have survived. Teachers often wish this adaptability allowed students to adapt to whatever methods the teacher used. However, the brain must maintain the function of protecting the individual from physical and psychological harm. Students cannot set aside the threat of psychological pain to adapt to a coercive classroom; to do so would mean they had sacrificed their autonomy, which is essential to a person's ability to adapt.

Teachers should only expect a partial carry over of the learning process from year to year. Every subsequent teacher must reestablish it. Assuming the amygdala was functioning to support memory, much of the information taught in previous years will carry forward. After just two or three years of school, students will quickly reestablish the habits of learning. Also, in as little as one year, students can make up two years of academic shortcomings. When teachers get the methods right, assessments at the end of the year will leave no doubt about what students have learned. However, if administrators have policies that prevent teachers from starting at the appropriate level, teachers should strongly object.

Concurrent with learning to listen, students need to learn to keep their eyes focused on their teacher when she is talking. Many students will allow their attention to drift. This problem will continue through the upper grades unless teachers make a point to develop each student's ability to focus their attention. They can accomplish this by interrupting the story or what she is talking about to praise those students who are looking at her.

Visual focus is a necessary skill for academic learning. Often teachers think their presentations have to be incredibly interesting to maintain student attention. That would be good, but is impossible for most teachers; however, all students can learn to focus. Like any other continuation behavior, teachers must reinforce the response while it is occurring. As in other situations, teachers will stop what they are saying and praise a few students for learning-related behavior. As in all situations, teachers should distribute their attention equally throughout the class.

The fact that many students in any class can already maintain visual attention on the teacher can be confusing. Teachers see some students maintaining their focus without being taught to; therefore, the behavior appears to be a developmental issue. Having some students who can maintain their focus is a major advantage to teachers, but they should never take the skill for granted. Teachers must remember that focusing is a behavior and behaviors can and must be taught.

Schools have always used seatwork as a method for students to practice new skills. As early as preschool and kindergarten, seatwork becomes an important avenue for learning. To maximize learning, students need to gradually become responsible for their own academic progress. In the upper grades, no one would disagree with the need for considerable seatwork activities; however, at the kindergarten level some teachers prefer to keep seatwork activities to a minimum. This choice does not alter the interactive teaching process. However, seatwork is important in the development of independent learning. When students learn to accept considerable responsibility for their own learning, greater achievement will soon follow. Cari starts seatwork on the first day of kindergarten and with the appropriate methodology begins developing students who can learn independently.

The process for getting the greatest results from seatwork is the same at all grade levels. The first issue will be to get some students started working. Even in a kindergarten class in an inner city school, some students will start work and try to follow instructions. Because some students are working, teachers have an avenue to get all students to work and to keep them working. By using differential social approval teachers can get an entire class to begin and continue to work.

This point frequently brings an objection. Teachers will argue that helping students continue working was the point of reinforcing students after 30 minutes of work. The problem was not with the teachers' intentions, but the fact that the process is ineffective for accomplishing the goal. Continuation behaviors must be reinforced while they are occurring.

The teacher will need to decide what work is appropriate for the class, but will sometimes find it necessary to provide easier material for some students. Of course individualizing instruction is more difficult, but students cannot maximize their potential unless they are working on the correct material for their academic level. In recent years, we have found many educators to be good at individualizing instruction.

To illustrate the process better, we will peek in on Cari teaching her students to work independently. When the first student picks up her pencil Cari will praise her. For instance she might say, "Jenny has her pencil. She is ready to start." This is said loud enough for all students to hear. She would then watch for another student to begin work. She immediately praises that student for whatever effort the student makes. A teacher wants to get as many students as possible to start working. This will inevitably require some individual help for some students. Even in the upper grades, students must be given the necessary help to get started. Too often we have found teachers want to ignore or fail students who do not do their work. Teachers cannot hope to reach their academic goals for the class unless all students make progress. Students cannot be taught to work by letting them fail. As we described previously, much can be lost and nothing gained by using negative consequences for failure to work. Punishment for failure to work may have a greater negative effect than punishment for inappropriate behavior.

Providing contingent social attention and withholding attention for nonproductive behavior — differential social attention — is an effective way to get students to engage in independent work. When a student starts working he must get recognition for his efforts. However, as more students begin working, the culture itself will encourage students to work. As students notice many other students working, it becomes the thing to do in that classroom. Also, as more students are working, students will find fewer opportunities to engage others in conversation. Once students are in the habit of working, fewer reinforcers will be necessary to keep them working. For students to maximize learning, they must continue to work almost constantly for the entire year. Obviously, upper grade students can work longer and more continuously than younger students; nevertheless, all students should learn to maximize their ability to work.

Continuously working is a major issue in getting all students to excel. Some teachers call this perseverance or the ability to do considerable amounts of work. Cari has found the word "perseverance" to be a bit hard for kindergarten students. Instead, she calls this "stamina." Cari frequently talks to her students about developing the stamina to work all day. This process is much the same as teaching any continuation behavior. First the student must be taught to work effectively for a few minutes. She then teaches students to extend those periods of work. Whenever she notices a student continuing to focus for a few minutes without looking away, she recognizes their effort by mentioning how they are developing the stamina to work constantly. Cari will say, "Marsha has been working so hard. She is developing stamina so she can learn as much as possible this year. Jared is working constantly, and he doesn't let anything distract him. Keep it up Shanee. You are building stamina." By remembering to praise students for working constantly, she can gradually, over a few weeks, improve student concentration. Students who learn to work most of the time will do better on achievement tests at the end of the year. Even at the preschool level students can learn to work continuously for several minutes without looking up.

For students to be effective at seatwork, students must keep working and move immediately from one response to the next. Students will sometimes write one word or make one letter and then take a break before moving on to the next word. If a student were to waste even a few seconds between words, he could waste a third or more of his work time per day. By the end of the year he would fall well short of his potential. The teacher must remind students not to take little daydreaming breaks. Nevertheless, the reminders will be of little value unless she also finds many opportunities to reinforce the nonstop work for every student.

For some students, praise itself will distract them. Having noticed this, some professionals have recommended never praising students.

However, critics should also notice that the same distraction can occur following anything said to students. Teachers cannot abandon essential aspects of learning because of a problem they can easily correct. When a teacher notices a student looking up following their interaction, she must treat the behavior the same way other minor issues are handled. The teacher will simply use differential social attention. Specifically, she will walk or turn away from the student who became distracted. However, when a student keeps working following a verbal interaction from the teacher, she will specifically praise the fact that he kept working. She may add a comment about how much she admires students who keep working without becoming distracted. Because of the power of differential social attention, students will soon learn to keep working. Teaching students to work constantly will be more difficult but still possible even with preschool children.

To excel, students must avoid distractions and work for long periods. However, the definition of a long period depends on the age and developmental levels of each student. For seatwork assignments, teachers can teach 25 or more students to work for long periods with only a few praises per minute. If every student had to be reinforced even once a minute, teachers would face the impossible task of praising 25 times per minute. Students learn to work for longer periods when a variable interval occurs between praise statements. In a previous chapter we discussed how teachers could never be perfectly consistent. However, when teachers use positive methods, some inconsistencies will benefit the outcome. When teachers are first teaching students to work independently, they should praise at a high rate of three to five times per minute. Fortunately, this rate of praise does not need to continue for the whole year. Most teachers will find that in just a few weeks one or two praises a minute will keep a normal class working for long periods. Teachers in the upper grades will find that more of their attention can be directed to academic accomplishments.

While students must learn to work constantly, their work must also be correct. As students build their work skills, they must simultaneously learn the importance of accuracy. Whether a kindergarten student is attempting to learn to make his letters, or a sixth grader is learning to write well-developed paragraphs, teachers must promote excellent work. Some students will almost automatically develop good work habits. Others, however, will take longer to develop that ability. Teachers can be thankful if they have even a few students who immediately understand the importance of accurate work. Teachers, by giving their recognition, so it can be heard by all students, can help nearly all students become consistently accurate.

One benefit of seatwork is that it is ideal for improving accuracy. During seatwork, teachers can move around and check students' work. They can encourage careful work, correct answers, and immediate corrections. Conversely, with homework, students have to return their work and it has to be checked when the teacher has time. Because of the delay between the time of the work and the feedback, learning to work accurately is obstructed.

A second issue is to teach students to work quickly. However, teachers cannot let students sacrifice accuracy for speed. Some students will never learn to work as quickly as others. Trying to pressure them into doing so may result in carelessness. The best way to do this is simply to watch for students as they improve their ability to work quickly. Some students who hear a teacher praise others for working quickly may sacrifice excellence so they can get attention for how much work they have completed. As a result teachers may want to make most of these praises very quietly to each student who is moving quickly through their work. When developing students' ability to increase the speed of their work, teachers must check enough of the work to be sure that accuracy is not being sacrificed.

Also, teachers can recognize students who are improving at working quickly without describing it. This is an instance where a general statement such as "good work" will reinforce the student for working accurately and quickly without having an unwanted effect on other students. Teachers should remember that giving approval to a student for making progress will result in continued progress even if it is only a fraction of what other students can do.

The problem of sacrificing accuracy for completing more work may become a significant problem in the upper grades. As students get into the upper grades and higher, the work load increases, making the issue of working quickly more important. Teachers must watch for and reinforce correct work being completed quickly. However, this can sometimes become tricky. If a teacher concentrates too much on working quickly, some students may become careless as they try to be the first one done. When other students hear a teacher praise a student for working quickly, or being the first one done, they may rush through their work. Teachers must take time to help students understand that nothing is more important than accuracy. Some students will take longer to complete their work than others. Because some students will work more slowly than others, teachers must be prepared to handle individual differences.

We have seen instances where the use of time limits causes some students to become careless. For instance, if students are expected to finish their multiplication tables in a set time, some students will hurry and fail to do their work correctly. When using time limits, teachers must take care to avoid increasing anxiety, or pushing students to inferior work. Only when students have mastered their facts is it time to encourage them to work more quickly; however, teachers must be careful that students always know that accuracy is most important.

Students need to learn to finish their work even if it takes them longer than other students. Teachers must focus some of their attention on the completion of seatwork. However, teachers must recognize a potential problem here too. If a teacher withholds her praise until students finish their work, some students will never build the necessary work habits. Consequently, many students will never learn to finish. A teacher who is trying to set really high expectations for students may unwittingly create failure, not success. While a teacher should admire the completion of assigned work, she must also recognize that she will need to help many students build those skills. Teachers must understand that the development of independent work skills is critical to accomplishing academic goals. In fact, work skills must be a central concern until every student is working very well. However, when we emphasize continuous work many teachers want to supplement the motivational techniques we've described with tangible reinforcers. Supplementing our methods with less powerful and countable reinforcers will weaken not strengthen the methodology. When teachers bring up this issue, we know they are not yet confident in the power of interactive methods. The most powerful process is to increase the number of social reinforcers. As supplemental motivation, some educators would suggest teachers simply structure more fun learning activities to follow seatwork. This is an acceptable practice. However, when a teacher structures such a sequence, she is not trying to use it as a contingency system so as to withhold any activities. All learning activities are important to all students; when some students are denied certain activities, their education has been adversely affected.

Given standard teaching methods, some students in the primary grades will conclude that they can never succeed in school. Unfortunately, most students who give up are both intelligent and capable. The problem is always the lack of one of four things: motivation, emotional regulation, self-confidence, or work-related skills. Some students do not have the work skills to match their intelligence. Teachers can build those skills, though not if they use a misguided technique of withholding reinforcers until the work is completed. That process will prevent some students from ever succeeding.

We have had teachers argue, "But that is only fair, they must learn to finish their work to earn reinforcers." Readers should understand that leaving some students behind forever is not a productive strategy. Withholding reinforcers is consistent with much of teacher training that, more than 40 years ago, became contingency based. A contingency-based system is any set of methods that delineates specific behaviors and the resulting reinforcers for those behaviors. By contrast our methods use social recognition for correct work and good effort. We frequently refer to our system as a non-countable reinforcement system. With our system, if the teacher is distributing her attention equally, students never try to keep track of how much attention they are receiving. A primary difference is that with contingency-based systems students soon come to consider the reinforcers more important than learning.

However, students must learn the work habits required to complete their work; withholding reinforcers for failing to finish will not teach what did not occur. The job of teachers is to advance all students, not just the best students. Nevertheless, most teachers have endorsed the management of events and activities to create contingent connections between the students' work and activities or small toys students can earn. However, activities will never match a teacher's attention as a powerful motivating factor. To realize the greatest motivational power, teachers need to manage their interactions to develop students who strive to succeed. For schools to achieve the results we are describing, they must identify the student behaviors that will lead to academic accomplishments and arrange for powerful reinforcers (such as social approval) to immediately follow those behaviors. However, that contingent reinforcer must follow many of those behaviors for every student; therefore, social approval is the only practical choice.

Besides building the behavior, social approval also builds the trust between student and teacher. Attempting to create a contingent relationship between everything the student likes and his behavior instead limits autonomy and creates distrust of the teacher. We think most teachers begin their careers expecting to help all students. However, without sufficient training to use positive social reinforcers, the results are often only marginally successful.

Despite the effectiveness of differential social approval, some students will be unable to do enough of their work to develop independent skills. Experienced teachers know that getting some students to even begin working will be difficult. For those students who have the least ability for independent work, motivational strategies may not be enough. Some students require more personal attention to do seatwork. Often they require personal help from a teacher or aide. While some students will need a little help getting started, others will require extensive help until they have developed more skills and confidence.

Many teachers will object: "If students get attention when they are not working they will never learn to work independently." This is a situation where theory has destroyed common sense. We acknowledge that some students may become helpless regarding school work. Nevertheless, teachers have no choice; students cannot learn if they do not work. Teachers cannot let a student sit for days or weeks without working. Teachers will find it useless to hope that negative consequences or withholding attention will miraculously have a positive effect in getting students to work independently. If differential social attention did not have a positive influence on work-related behaviors in just a few hours, another solution must be found.

Some students will require constant help before they can meet seat-work expectations. This might require an aide, a floating teacher, or help from a sixth grade student. Despite the risk that a student might become dependent on individual help, teachers have no choice; they cannot let students fail.

Once helplessness has developed, much work will be required to develop the student's ability to manage his own work. Usually a skilled teacher will be needed to wean the student from his dependence on constant help. Success can be accomplished through a series of techniques, with each successive step dependent on the previous step being successful several times. First, the teacher who is helping the child will begin by occasionally redirecting her attention for just a moment. This may need to be so brief the student barely notices. Art will frequently have the teacher say to the student, "Great. You kept working on your own, even when I turned away." A teacher can use such a statement even if the student never noticed her turning away.

The second step has two parts. The teacher tells the student to do something he has previously learned. She also says, "I'll be back in a moment." At the beginning of this phase she steps away for literally one second. Gradually, she increases the length of time the student works independently. One teacher had increased this time span to about three minutes when the student said to her, "You can help other students. I don't need that much help now." Art knows of several cases where after weeks or even months of one-on-one help, students learned to work independently and at least some became superior students.

Many teachers find they must learn to direct a good portion of their attention to those who are trying and improving. Mrs. Bradford, a sixth grade teacher, accomplished much of what we advocate. Students were working on a math seatwork assignment. Following is a sample of her approval statements. "Mary is working hard. John is nearly finished with his paper. Donita is rechecking her paper." Quietly she said to Sam, "Keep up the hard work, you are improving." She continued, "Jason is taking his time and trying to be neat." She bent over to check some of Karen's work. Mrs. Bradford quietly asked Karen to go back and correct three of her problems that she had marked as needing to be corrected. By late in the school year, her students were consistently working at a pace that allowed them to finish with accurate and neat work. The students had learned the skills early in the year and maintained them with little effort from the teacher.

Developing Higher Academic Functions

Simple work-related behavior will not be enough in the upper grades. Teachers will have to give considerable attention to other issues. Students will need to learn to read for meaning. Among other tasks they will need to know how to find a topic sentence and describe the topic in their own words. In math, word problems will be especially hard for some students; therefore teachers will want to teach them how to turn word problems into simple numerical problems they can solve. Most upper grade teachers will not have trouble transferring these methods to the lessons they are teaching.

Once older students have learned to work and contribute to the good of the group, a teacher will need to step back and let them work. Upper grade students might resent a teacher who praises too much. However, every student will be different; a teacher cannot justify withholding attention from some students just because they are sixth graders. Students will let teachers know what they need. As students develop self-confidence and a desire to learn, they will need less praise.

Once many students, whether in primary or upper grades, are completing their work accurately, teaching becomes easier. Students have established the foundation for an important attribute — self-motivation. Sometimes even with young students self-motivation looks almost like an acquired need or motivational drive to excel. When students are driven to excel, their lives may change forever; nevertheless, during the first few years this newly acquired attribute is fragile. Teachers using ill-advised methods can destroy that motivation. The most destructive methods are typically forms of negative consequences or threats of consequences. Teachers must be careful not to destroy the attribute that will ensure success. Once students can set goals and motivate themselves to achieve those goals, teachers are more like mentors. In contrast, when teachers are the driving force, they may feel like they are pulling a sled full of students through the snow. However, once many students in a class are motivated to excel, the students, not the teachers, provide the force that propels learning.

Most teachers admire self-motivated students. Unfortunately, the process by which self-motivation develops has not been well understood. The question is, how can schools take students who must be externally motivated and help them become self-motivated? One could ask, "Is there a specific method that develops the attribute?" The answer is, "We have already described the methods." Teachers will not find one special technique to develop motivation, but instead must use all the skills already described to encourage enhancement of self-motivation. Once students have developed the ability to learn by working independently, they need continued encouragement and recognition for accomplishments.

We see it starting with kindergarten students and continuing to develop through high school. We have had many teachers argue that self-motivation cannot emerge at such a young age. However, we routinely see kindergarten students working beyond anything teachers envisioned. For instance Jana, mentioned in previous chapters, had to scramble to provide enough work to keep her kindergarten students working the last two months of the school year. Developing self-motivation is not dependent on additional methods, but is in part dependent on the teacher maintaining the system and never giving up on the process.

As students become better at listening, remembering, and following instructions they are on their way to becoming self-motivated. With these behaviors in place, students will recognize that they are constantly learning. They come to understand, possibly while they are still in kindergarten, that the teacher is more of a facilitator of learning, and they are not dependent on her for all knowledge. They may develop an unquenchable thirst for knowledge. During this development, students — eventually, but not immediately — learn an untaught lesson: they personally hold the key to their success. When this lesson is learned, they know that neither criticism from another student nor a correction from a teacher can stop their drive to succeed. Their self-motivation is no longer fragile.

Students will not become self-motivated from being told how important it is. If this attribute does not develop when expected, the only choice is to continue high levels of differential social attention for independent work. Because self-motivation is an attribute, the only way it can develop is by teaching behaviors that transform students from pursuing external rewards to working for the self-satisfaction of accomplishment. As students become more able to work independently, teachers can gradually reduce the number of social reinforcers. However, a word of caution: when teachers reduce their rate of verbal approval, they must be sure students do not interpret this as apathy regarding their work. Teachers must always show enthusiasm for students' work and cannot justify reducing the level of social attention because they expect them to become self-motivated. Only when the attribute is evident, is less praise needed.

The Academic Gap Between Students

A major concern in education is that some students will be left behind while others move further and further ahead. One job of teachers is to help all students learn as much as possible. When slower students are making good progress, they will partially reduce the gap. However, a necessary part of the solution is to individualize instruction. For teachers to individualize instruction, they need students to work independently. Establishing a culture of responsible independence will do much of this work. The students will provide much of the solution.

We have seen teachers, at all levels, go from pushing students through the curriculum to trying to keep up with students demanding more work. Not all students will reach that level at the same moment, but once enough students develop the desire to learn, teachers will be hard pressed to provide enough work. Like Jana, at least the first time they encounter this drive to accomplish, teachers may find themselves scrambling to challenge the better students and simultaneously help others with the remedial work they need. Some teachers may need more help from administrators than ever before. However, this is the kind of problem administrators want to have.

Following is one of our favorite examples. It was near the beginning of a school year and Eva Krahn had a student in her fifth grade class who forgot his homework for the third day in a row. She was being as pleasant as any teacher could. Other teachers told her, "That is your problem, you keep giving him chances. Give the papers an F and go on. He must learn to be responsible."

She recognized the truth in the last part of the statement. Sammy did need to become more responsible. She also knew that getting students to become responsible is complicated and punishing failure would not help. To create success, she would need to build his academic skills. This would require that she find ways to make him successful so he could become more self-confident. Improved confidence would pave the way for greater responsibility. Teachers recognize that students from homes where parents are highly involved with their children's education almost invariably do better in school. As a result, teachers often shift the blame for students' failure to the parents. Nevertheless, students can attain success in school even when parents do not do their part. Teachers can and must help students learn despite their home situation. Eva was not going to allow Sammy to fail because his parents would not or could not help. At the end of the school day she said, "Sammy, I need to talk to you for a moment."

He came to her desk with his head down and said, "What, Miss Krahn?"

Eva said, "For the last few days you have forgotten your homework. I want to find some way to help you remember." Readers should notice that she did not threaten consequences. She wanted her student, over time, to come to understand that the natural consequence is that he will not learn as much as his classmates. She knew she would have to help him remember.

Sammy said, "I know, but I can't remember."

Eva replied, "Of course you can. What's your name?"

Sammy said, "Sammy."

Eva said, "Sammy who?"

Sammy answered, "Sammy Irwin."

"When is your birthday, Sammy?"

"July 17."

Eva asked him three or four more questions and he answered them all correctly. She said, "See, you can remember lots of things. I think you can remember your homework."

Sammy responded, "I'm not very good at homework."

Eva answered, "That's okay. It is my job to help you get good at school work. But if I never see your homework I can't help you. Please do as much as you can and bring it to school."

Sammy said, "Okay."

He did not bring his homework the next day. Eva again talked to him after school. He again said he would bring it the next day. However, the next morning, he did not have his homework. Eva would not give up. She talked to him after school. Finally, after four days of reminding him he brought his homework. He had it about half done. She expressed her appreciation for him bringing his work.

Sammy said, "But it isn't very good."

She answered, "Remember, we said if you bring it, I will help you do it better."

After school she spent three minutes helping him understand his homework assignment. He had to catch the bus, so that is all the time they had. Over the school year, he only forgot his homework a few more times. It took most of the first semester with Eva helping one to three days a week. Sometimes this was during class time, after school, or during recess. At the end of the year he scored just over the 50th percentile on his end-of-year achievement test. That was lower than average for her class, but by the end of the school year Sammy believed he could learn. He wanted to learn.

This success did not just happen. Eva had to work at creating it. If she had tried using negative consequences to coerce Sammy into bringing his homework to school, she would have forced him into a resistance that may have resulted in him barely passing fifth grade. Sammy responded positively to the hope of success; he would not have to fear of failure. Failing him would have only resulted in more serious academic problems. The result may not seem earth shattering, but Eva helped him develop confidence and interest in learning. Some readers might miss that Sammy's success probably had a positive impact on how well other students did that year. Anything that affects one student affects every student. A teacher's responsibility is to help students first master the skills required to learn and then to learn. A student must receive recognition for being successful at learning before he can develop a desire to learn.

With proper development many students will develop a desire to achieve. They will become the teacher's greatest asset in getting more students to want to learn. While some students will develop the attribute in a few months, others will take longer. Even with interactive teaching, some students who experience greater difficulty in learning may not develop this attribute until the second or even third year. By systematically directing social approval to every student for the advancements they make, learning will take on a characteristic much like a hunger for food. The student will pursue learning.

Question and Answer

Question: I am an elementary school principal. I sometimes get frustrated with teachers who make excuses about students being unable to learn. I tell them that the students can learn more than they think, but it never helps. What can I do to help teachers stop making excuses.

Answer: You obviously care deeply about the success of all students. Unfortunately, by taking that approach you have set up a situation where some teachers are determined to prove you wrong. Your teachers may continually come up with new reasons why their students cannot learn. Our suggestion is for you to recognize those teachers who do achieve excellent results with their students. Have those teachers describe their techniques. You can help the best teachers articulate the reasons for their success and get your teachers to celebrate the success of every teacher. Introduce your teachers to this book and some will soon develop these skills. If you can create a culture where teachers are free to vocalize their success, the culture will do the work. Because of your dedication, you are trying to pull some teachers to the summit. For reasons we may never know, some are dragging their feet. You want to create a culture where teachers admire each other for their commitment to effective teaching.

You need your teachers to take themselves to the summit. Be sure to notice the first steps and milestones along the way.

Summary

- Every student needs to develop a desire to learn.
- Every student can achieve to the level of his ability.
- The entire class must work together to help each other excel.
- Every student needs to develop the behaviors that lead to academic accomplishments.
- Helping students learn will depend on using correct interactive methods.
- A teacher should be evaluated on how well she does with all students.
- Listening, remembering, and focusing are behaviors students learn when teachers reinforce those behaviors.

Effective Interactions Teachers Must Use and Why

Effective Teacher Interactions	Rationale
Ask questions to find out if students are listening.	Teachers can only know if students were listening when students answer questions correctly.
Express social approval to students for listening.	Remember, social approval is the universal reinforcer for students.
Reinforce correct answers when students remember what they hear.	To learn, students must remember.
Reinforce students for maintaining their focus on the teacher.	Students cannot learn if they are distracted.
Have students do seatwork as a form of practice.	Students learn by doing. Much of what they need to learn can be practiced while working independently. Seatwork helps students take responsibility for their learning.
Teachers will need to express their social approval hundreds of times to develop productive independent work.	Persistence at a continuation behavior is learned when it is frequently reinforced over extended periods. ☞

Effective Interactions	Rationale
Some students will require help before they can learn to work.	A student must begin working to learn to work.
Sometimes it is necessary to give students lots of help for extended periods of time. This could result in students becoming dependent on this help. Nevertheless, the teacher has no choice.	Students must learn to work before they can learn to work independently.
When students become dependent on help, address it by repeatedly describing how others are working independently.	Most likely the culture will do the work.
For students who work, create short periods of independent work. Express approval for that work. Get other students to celebrate a student's independent work.	When the culture does not do the work, the teacher must get the students to work and reinforce the behavior.
Teach students to work quickly, but never sacrifice accuracy.	Inaccuracy is the worst enemy of learning.

Interactions Teachers Should Avoid and Why

Ineffective Interactions	Rationale
Negative consequences for failure to work will not be effective in developing productive academic behavior.	Positive behaviors can only be developed by getting students to engage in those behaviors and reinforcing those behaviors.
Teachers cannot ignore for lengthy periods a student who is not working.	If a student is not working, withholding a reinforcer will not help.

7
Coercion and Positive Alternatives in Classrooms

I N THE FIRST SIX CHAPTERS we have described much of a new methodology, its scientific foundation, and the results educators should expect from adopting these methods. The methods we describe are not that difficult to learn, but our experience has been that the change will be difficult for some teachers. When teachers have spent most of their career using traditional methods, they may find it difficult to adopt new methods. However, many students will not be successful until effective methods are adopted. Sometimes we encounter teachers who are willing to adopt some positive methods, but insist they must continue to use systems of consequences for inappropriate behavior. Unfortunately, the positive results described in previous chapters can only be realized when coercive methods are discontinued. In part this chapter will describe the disadvantages of several intervention methods common in our schools. The authors discussed whether this chapter was even necessary, but eventually decided that many teachers would be reluctant to give up coercive methods unless we explicitly describe how they affect students.

A major obstacle in elementary education, especially in the primary grades, is disruptive behavior. Many teachers find their students becoming disruptive to the point of interfering with teaching and learning. When students are talking without permission, out of their seats, bickering with each other, pushing, shoving, crowding, arguing, and insulting others, teaching is nearly impossible. Elementary teachers are familiar with these behaviors. The difficulty they pose may be hard to imagine until one has encountered several students engaging in such behavior simultaneously. Undergraduate and graduate courses are dedicated to behavior management, and many books have been written on the subject. Teachers go to seminars and take website training, all with little benefit. The theories for behavior management systems are numerous; however, the problems persist. Teachers are doing the best they can, with traditional methods, to manage classroom behavior.

It would be unthinkable to argue that education and learning could succeed with all the disruptions, distractions, and turmoil that fill many classrooms. However, teachers will struggle if they look to coercive methods for solutions. By opting for a positive methodology, teachers can solve the behavior problems in classrooms.

Many behavior management techniques teachers use depend on elaborate systems of consequences and warnings for inappropriate behavior. These procedures are designed to warn students of impending consequences for misbehavior. Many educators consider consequences and warnings to represent a sound theory. Unfortunately, the method is not very effective in any situation and destructive in group environments. Most educators are a little unsure why the procedures are much less effective than the theory would suggest. The intent of consequences is to dissuade students from making bad choices. According to the theory, students who encounter such consequences, will refrain from engaging in such behavior — a simple warning will hopefully serve to dissuade them from more serious misbehavior.

Teachers and administrators usually contend these methods work for some students but nothing works for others. If these procedures worked for all students, the alternate methods presented in previous chapters would only apply to academic accomplishments. In any given class, some students will behave very well whatever process is used. Teachers then assume the blame for poor behavior lies with the students, parents, or some aspect of our culture. District offices, school administrators, and teachers continue to recommend and use standard methods. We will examine some consequence-based procedures and explain them in the light of the science described in Chapter Two.

Systems of Warnings and Consequences

Rene Baxter was with her third grade class. The group was typical for the demographics of the area. In this case, an observer was in the classroom and provided her assessment. She was familiar with schools that had more difficult students to educate. As she looked around the room, she noticed it was attractive. Rene had displayed charts, materials, projects from students, and decorations, making the room tastefully arranged and inviting. The observer did notice a large stoplight chart on the front wall. A separate clothes pin was assigned to each student by name. This was a system for warning and informing students of their misbehavior. The names of all students were clustered on green for the beginning of the day.

Rene was teaching multiplication. She asked, "Lynn, what is three times three?" Lynn was unsure of the answer. She paused for a moment and Rene waited patiently.

Finally, Lynn answered, "Eight?"

Rene replied, "No, think harder."

The pause continued and Lynn became more anxious. Some students seemed impatient with the pause and others apparently were relieved that they were not the ones on the spot. Two boys near the back of the class were quietly talking. This was apparently within the teacher's tolerance. Then one boy giggled aloud. Rene immediately said, with some aggravation, "Bryan, move your name to yellow."

He looked disgusted. The talking stopped. The other boy immediately refocused his attention to the teacher. Bryan got up from his seat and slowly moved to the front of the room. He reluctantly moved his name to yellow. As he returned to his seat, he walked out and around, pausing for a moment to look at something on a table. Bryan took nearly two minutes to make the round trip to the stoplight chart and back.

Finally Rene asked another student to answer the question first posed to Lynn. Sarah instantly said, "Three times three is nine." Rene acknowledged the correct answer. This part of the lesson continued for several more minutes. During this time she told two more students to move their names to yellow. The intervention always immediately stopped the behavior. The observer noticed that when students moved their name they took a long time getting back to their seat.

Following the oral review of multiplication tables, the teacher had a student hand out multiplication worksheets to students. During the seatwork activity, Rene responded to minor inappropriate behavior by having a few more students move their name to yellow. By this point, Bryan was on red and the teacher told him that he would have a note to take home to his parents. Bryan was apparently unfazed by this. Our observer concluded, and later verified, that he had been on red often during the year. As the morning continued, Rene became more agitated at having to deal with misbehavior. The observer was often confused about why some students were told to move their name when nothing was said to others who behaved the same way. Sometimes, the teacher ignored identical or more disruptive behavior. Readers will remember how inconsistencies in the use of negative consequences with animals was linked to behavior similar to insanity in humans. Given the methods used in this classroom, ignoring inappropriate behavior had no chance of being effective. Ignoring is not a stand-alone technique. It is only effective when used as a part of differential social approval.

In the previous chapter, we discussed the problems with inconsistent consequences. Because classrooms are such complex environments, teachers cannot possibly be totally consistent. The methods advocated in this book will be effective despite inevitable inconsistencies. One should expect success only if many instances of appropriate behavior are reinforced. However, when teachers expertly use the process we describe, fewer instances of needing to deal directly with problem behavior will arise. The difference is that teachers will help students strive to control their impulsive emotional and behavioral responses themselves. Once a student is striving to maintain control, each instance of success will bring him closer to emotional regulation. When teachers master the interactive teaching process, they may see significant progress in just a few days.

When Rene told a student to move his name, the observer also watched how the other students reacted. Some students were apprehensive. Perhaps they were concerned about whether they too would get a consequence. However, some students may have considered it a challenge — could they violate the rule and escape the consequence?

Sometimes she noticed students snickering at others for being in trouble. The teacher never addressed this reaction. Once, the observer noticed, a student delighted that another boy was in trouble. The appropriate way to handle such behavior would be for the teacher to explain: "Everyone is expected to respect each other and help other students remember how we behave in class." Once the appropriate behavior is occurring, the teacher can reinforce the behavior.

Subsequent observations in other classrooms revealed Rene's application of the stoplight system to be typical. Usually at the end of the day any student whose indicator was on green earned a trip to a prize box. Students always look forward to selecting a prize. However, the privilege is based on a teacher's subjective evaluation of a student's behavior. In previous chapters, we described that a reinforcer can only strengthen a behavior that occurred immediately before the reinforcer. A prize at the end of the day cannot develop any of the behaviors necessary for behaving appropriately all day. At best, a prize can slightly help those students who have the self-discipline to maintain appropriate behavior throughout the day. The prize cannot help students develop the behaviors required to self-discipline their classroom actions. As a result the privilege has virtually no impact on improving student behavior. Most typically, once a student is on red, he has no chance to return to green and is not allowed to choose from the prize box. Such a student has no reason to attempt to improve his behavior for the remainder of the day. Schools need methods that will: (1) constantly motivate students to exhibit their best behavior; (2) constantly motivate students to inhibit inappropriate behavior. An effective motivational system for classrooms must include these essential characteristics, without the use of negative stimuli, which even if they had a small effect in reducing inappropriate behavior, would interfere with learning.

At best, a delayed reinforcement system provides slight encouragement to the best students to remain on green. While students start on green, the system is primarily a warning system for students to discontinue certain classes of behavior. However, the effect would not be consistent with all students. For those students who need the most help to improve their classroom behavior, the system is a constant source of apprehension. Even many students who are doing well, much of the time, report being nervous about the possibility of being put on yellow. This anxiety that students experience interferes with memory in two ways. First, new information may never receive the appropriate emotional tag necessary for it to be remembered. Second, stress may prevent the recall of previously learned material. Those students who most need help in reducing stress will experience the most stress and their academic accomplishments will be even more adversely affected.

We find the same students finish on red nearly every day. Many parents, teachers, and administrators recognize this. Also, teachers usually find it necessary to use red more often as the school year continues. These observations suggest stoplight systems are not effective and the science we have described explains the reasons. Besides the neuropsychological issues, negative consequences are better at getting people to avoid situations than eliminate misbehavior. Teachers must teach students to behave appropriately; therefore, even if teachers have an effective process for reducing inappropriate behavior, they would still need to develop the behavior necessary for learning.

Teachers use a stoplight system with the intention of discouraging particular students from certain behaviors. However, despite this intent, the process is not very effective. Furthermore, neuroscience explains how the memory of some students will be adversely affected and others may develop pathological reactions. The third fundamental says that anything that affects one student will affect all students. Observation, experience, and interviews with students would suggest adverse effects from systems based on consequences. Nevertheless, scientists have not conducted studies to show the side effects and possible damage from the use of such systems.

The most important job of all teachers is to promote academic excellence. To be successful, they must be aware of the emotional and behavioral impact of their systems. Educators cannot afford to be wrong about the effects on students. Years ago, with the adoption of consequence systems for behavior management, teachers were taught to ignore any emotional response from students. The assumption was that the behavior was the only thing that mattered. This was, however, based on interpretations of scientific studies, not the findings per se. In the last 20 years, research in neuropsychology has made it clear that emotions are a critical part of all learning. Educators cannot allow their good intentions to skew their perception of what is actually happening with students. For maximum effectiveness teachers must be sensitive to how their actions influence all students.

We are fully aware that stoplight systems are fixtures in many elementary classrooms. Often administrators recommend teachers use them for managing behavior. However, they impede learning for many students and possibly even for some whose indicator is always on green. The system is not consistent with what is known about human behavior and the results do not validate its methods. Because alternative methods are not well known, schools continue to use coercive methods. While stoplight systems or similar methods may impede education, their elimination may or may not improve what is happening in classrooms. Any subsequent improvement will depend on using positive methods to increase productive behavior.

Coercive interventions in response to common childhood mistakes erode students' self-confidence, exactly the opposite of what teachers want to accomplish. The best academic advancements are associated with greater self-confidence. Unfortunately, the use of coercive and consequence-based systems can destroy much that teachers accomplish in classrooms.

Group Punishment

Many teachers use group punishment systems. For example, several students had not completed their assigned work. The teacher decided to keep all students in from recess, in the hope that the consequence would "teach" students to get their work done. The logic does not hold up. Negative consequences cannot increase work-related behaviors but will have a negative affect on the students' trust of the teacher. Remember, anything that affects one student affects every student, which is the exact intent of group punishment. The point the teacher missed is that for most students nothing good could come from a group consequence. Our conclusion is that this teacher was willing to "hurt" most students in the hope of helping some. If research were conducted on the effects of group punishment, we would expect no benefits to be found in educational situations. Even if punishment could reduce the frequency of some behaviors, the consequence would have to immediately follow the specific behavior of specific students. Failure of some students to finish their work is a result of inefficient work-related behavior. The only solution is to build that behavior; therefore, teachers must reinforce the desired work habits.

We expect one objection to our criticism of group punishment to be directed at our advocacy of a common purpose. Someone may argue that if students are expected to work together, then they should expect to suffer together when the group does not succeed. Perhaps teachers hope other students will exert peer pressure to get certain students to work harder. When a teacher's coercion does not work, expecting coercion from students to work is unreasonable. Getting students to complete their work is beyond the reach of other students. Helping students learn to complete their work is not dependent on eliminating nonproductive behaviors, but instead on developing productive behaviors.

The Happy/Sad Face Chart

A teacher we know was told by her assistant principal to start a happy/sad face system in her class. She told her assistant principal that they could talk about it later. She prepared the following paragraphs and gave it to the assistant principal.

> I would never use a happy/sad face chart. I am never upset with a student or sad about how students behave. As a teacher, I constantly and objectively assess whether the behavior I am seeing is beneficial to or impeding the individual and group goals. For those behaviors that are benefiting the common cause, I will decide if it needs to be strengthened or if it is well developed. If it needs strengthening, I will praise a student exhibiting the behavior. If it is impeding the student's progress or the group's efforts, I will make a mental note to find

opportunities to strengthen the corresponding positive behavior when it occurs. Furthermore, if I found myself irritated, I would never remain irritated for more than a second. To do so would be counterproductive in pursuit of our common objectives. So a sad face could never remain up for more than one second.

Two more points need to be mentioned: 1. The student involved would have to know precisely what he or she had done that disappointed me. Otherwise it would be useless in producing change, and instead would adversely affect the students' trust of me. 2. The chart would be distracting and confusing to other students. When it is sometimes necessary to intervene directly with misbehavior, I do it gently and with a rationale for the appropriate behavior in the situation. The rationale must also describe how inappropriate behavior affects the class. With such an intervention, I must succeed in creating appropriate behavior for a few minutes so I can strengthen the desired class of behaviors. As often as not, when I see behavior that is counterproductive, I am admittedly sad for a moment because it is in part my fault. When a student is disruptive, I might be sad at myself for having failed to have developed the appropriate behavior.

Her note says it perfectly. Readers should also note that she considered it her responsibility to develop appropriate student behavior. The use of such charts has a negative affect on students and prevents uniting them for a common purpose.

The Home Note

Keeping parents informed about their children's behavior is necessary. Parents do not like being blindsided months later about how their child has been behaving in school. Unfortunately, problems invariably arise. The process is not as simple as it seems.

Many teachers use notes almost exclusively to report problem behavior. One problem with this application is that students behave appropriately much of the time. Reporting only the inappropriate behavior to parents distorts the truth. When parents get a home note describing some problem every few days, they do not get a clear perspective on what is happening. Even the more difficult students engage in hundreds of appropriate behaviors per day, but parents are seldom told about a student's good behavior. Also, when parents get a note they feel they should do something. They want to make the teacher understand they do not approve of their child's behavior. Teachers expect that reaction from parents; they want the parent to feel obligated to punish the child for the behavior problem. Frequently, teachers advise parents that consequences are necessary to improve the child's behavior. As already described, punitive consequences do not work very well in reducing problem behavior. When punishment is used hours later, it is destructive. Parents would presumably explain to their child that he is being punished for something he did hours earlier, but such explanations are useless. When punishment is delayed several hours, the primary result is to damage the relationship between parent and child. Unfortunately, punishment will seldom reduce the frequency of the target behavior. Instead of continuing with systems that do not work, we developed systems that will produce the change schools want.

The protocol in interactive teaching is to report a serious behavior issue to parents and tell them how we handled the issue. We further advise parents that additional consequences would do more harm than good. Unfortunately, many parents will punish their child anyway. In our experience, when issues must be reported to parents it needs to be done in person with the child present. We describe to parents how the problem was handled. Telling parents, with the child present, not to use any additional consequences is sometimes successful. We recognize this is difficult when children ride a bus and parents cannot get in that day. Our advice is simple; use positive methods to promote appropriate behavior and avoid the problem.

Another version of the home note is to report to parents every day. Usually the system involves evaluating a student on three to five areas. Typically, a three-level evaluation is used. Most frequently, the categories are excellent, acceptable, and unacceptable. In some ways, this is better than the red card system. However, concerning the system's shortcoming, Art calls this a global assessment. Children engage in hundreds, even thousands of behaviors every day. The note combines many behaviors into a single (global) assessment. Any assessment that tries to sum up large amounts of behavior into a single category cannot possibly provide any useful information. (This would be like describing the weather on earth for a particular day as hot or cold.) Such an assessment is so broad that it has little meaning regarding practical issues. Even the person assigning the assessment would have difficulty specifying enough details to warrant the assessment.

A parent who reads on a home note that her daughter needs to improve on work habits in school cannot do anything about it at home. The problem occurred in a classroom and must be addressed in class. To build appropriate work behavior, a reinforcer must occur during the continuation of the response. Parents can have very little influence on their child's behavior in class. However, reporting to parents what is being done to improve the child's work habits would be useful. Subsequent reports on how the teacher's efforts were working would be appropriate, because they keep the parent informed without transferring the responsibility away from the environment where the problem is occurring.

Many systems used in education were designed as punishment systems and therefore undermine attempts by teachers to develop appropriate behavior. However, even systems developed to reinforce appropriate behavior frequently have major flaws. A typical flaw is to use reinforcers that can be easily counted at the end of the day; they usually create competition among students. Another flaw is that teachers often use these countable systems to show favoritism to certain students.

The Purple Card System

A first grader was talking to his dad about school. He was happy about having gotten a purple card.

The dad responded, "That is apparently a good thing."

His son said, "If I get four more, I'll get to pick something from the prize box."

Dad said, "Is this the first time you've gotten a purple card?"

His son answered, "Yes."

Given that it was nearly halfway through the school year his dad asked, "Have other students gotten purple cards?"

His son quickly showed his irritation, "Well yes, but that's the thing. Two other students have gotten purple cards, but it's not fair."

Dad asked, "Why isn't it fair?"

The boy answered, "There are four of us who are the best students in class. We are the best at our lessons and in how we behave. The others are Brock, Jenny, and Amber. Brock has two purple cards, I have one, Amber doesn't have any, but Jenny has 21. It's not fair because we should all have about the same number, because we are all about the same in class."

His sister, who was in the third grade said, "When I'm a teacher, I will never use a card system."

Dad asked, "Why not?"

The boy's sister continued, "I have never known my brother to be envious. But he is envious of Jenny. I wouldn't want some of my students to be envious of others. I would want every student to feel important."

If readers are wondering, these are direct quotations and Art verified the story by talking to the children directly. Even a student who was not in the class could see the effect on other students. However, other issues need to be mentioned. The card system is designed to reinforce good behavior. However, apparently by late November, only a couple dozen behaviors were worth being reinforced. Despite the intent, developing the desired classroom behavior requires recognition for hundreds of appropriate behaviors per day; therefore, an assessment at the end of the day is useless. Whether intentionally or not, the system was being used to play favorites. When other students see a teacher playing favorites they lose trust in the teacher and the academic performance of many students will be adversely affected. The conduct behavior of some students may also be affected.

A student becoming envious is a result of the dual effects of countable reinforcers and the fact that anything that happens to one student will affect all students in the class. Expecting several students to be envious would be reasonable. In this case, where Art was able to interview the student, the process apparently did not affect his academic performance. He was at the top of the class. However, at least some parents thought the overall performance of the class was lower than it could have been. Because of the fundamentals of groups, it would be surprising if other adverse effects were not present. Unfortunately, we have noticed that many teachers are not concerned about how other students are reacting.

Our connection to this class was the student, not the teacher; we could not interview other students to know how they were affected. Perhaps, instead of becoming envious some became resentful of the teacher. Most will develop a mistrust for her because she plays favorites and is not fair. For other students, the envy may grow to hatred of the teacher or even of Jenny. Teachers must be aware that whatever influences one student will affect every student. Art has seen the effects of teachers playing favorites several other times, and the results are never good. Teachers must use systems that will have positive effects throughout the group. However, readers should also understand that with this system, the time between receiving the card and the exchange is so long that no reinforcing value is possible.

Tangible reinforcement systems, or any reinforcement system primarily dependent on using tangible reinforcers, have three things in common. First, the time to develop the system of what behaviors will be reinforced and the reinforcer used to strengthen those behaviors would be hard to justify unless it was very effective. Every intervention takes time that could be better used. Teachers have a difficult and time-consuming job; any recommended methods should be the most efficient means to a productive end. A specific social reinforcer takes less than a second to complete; delivering a token or any tangible reinforcer will take at least five to ten seconds. The result is almost always the same — teachers will not use enough tangible reinforcers to accomplish the objective. But even if they did, they would spend an hour per day just giving reinforcers to students. A second issue is that the store of items must be regularly re-stocked. The third issue is that these systems are less effective than using a primary reinforcement system. They also have unwanted effects on both the targeted student and the class. Often we see students becoming more concerned about earning reinforcers than the responses they are intended to strengthen. Moreover, a few five-to-ten-seconds interruptions will destroy the culture of students constantly working to learn as much as they can learn. These factors, which are universally associated with tangible reinforcement methods, make the application futile. Instead, teachers need systems like those we described in previous chapters that get students to take more responsibility for their own behavior and simultaneously have a beneficial effect across all students.

We have described how coercion adversely affects students and entire classes. We recognize that teachers will be faced with difficult behavior, but every teacher has alternatives for how to handle inappropriate conduct. However, teachers have for the most part never been trained in the necessary methods. The remainder of this chapter will describe how students respond when a teacher uses more positive methods to handle problem behavior.

Positive Alternatives

One year, in the middle of January, Cari got word from her principal that a new student would be joining her kindergarten class. This was not a surprise. She knew another teacher was having considerable difficulty with the boy. This teacher was using a stoplight system and home notes; nevertheless, the behavior of the class and especially of the boy had continued to get worse since the beginning of the year. The principal, Mrs. Anderson, had asked Cari about moving him to her class. Cari had agreed. The hope was that by getting the worst offender out of that class, the others would improve. The problem is not unique; in this, and many other Title 1 schools, some students exhibit very serious behavior.

She announced to her class that they would be getting a new classmate, and his name is Ben. Some students recognized the name. One girl asked, "Is he bad?" They had seen him lose privileges and sit against the wall during recess.

Cari explained to her class, "He is having a little trouble following rules. We have been given the privilege of helping him remember." Many teachers would have worried about adding a difficult student to their class. While an additional student would add to her workload, she was not concerned about his behavior. Over the years, administrators have transferred many difficult students into her class and she had a perfect record with them. The boy was a child and the class was a group; therefore, his success was assured. The only question was, how successful?

About ten minutes later Ben arrived. He was greeted and welcomed to class. Cari started by reviewing the rules and having students introduce themselves. Every few seconds she would reinforce some students for obeying the rules. She had students explain how, in this class, we all help each other do better.

Following introductions the class started work, and she reinforced several students for following the rules. A few times per minute, she would identify a student and describe his good behavior. "Jackie is remembering to raise her hand when she needs help. Brandon is sitting and working hard." In recent months, her students had behaved so well, she had seldom praised students for appropriate conduct behavior. Recently, most of her attention had been directed toward good work habits, neatness, and persistence. She expected this shift of focusing on behavior issues to be short lived. Cari fully expected the boy would soon be following most rules.

She made a point to catch Ben being good every few minutes. She said, "Ben, is keeping his hands to himself." When they went to math centers, she had students explain what Ben needed to do. Heather said, "We always push our chair in, so walking through is easier for everyone." Brandon said, "We walk quietly and straight to math centers. Then we find a place to sit." Mrs. Williams asked another student to be his buddy for a few days and help him learn the new routine. She could have done this herself, and sometimes she would, but this was a way to help other students become invested in Ben's success. The more successful he was, the more other students would learn during the remainder of the year.

Sometimes during the next month the other students started encouraging Ben. They would say to him, "That's the way to walk in line. Thank you for hanging up your coat. You are following the playground rules, good for you." Cari had not prompted students to do this, but they had learned to help each other improve. The praise was natural, because they wanted their class to succeed.

This process, directed toward assuring Ben's success, continued almost constantly for two weeks. Only a few times did Cari need to stop what she was doing and deal with Ben's problem behavior. However, she had noticed that several times another student would stop Ben and explain how to behave in their class. Once a girl, Judi, explained to Ben, "When you yell at Cassandra, it hurts her feelings and disrupts the whole class."

Ben replied, "I don't care."

Judi said, "We all care because it helps us learn."

Ben looked at Judi as if she were from another planet and said, "I don't care about nobody."

Judi said, "We care about you."

After three weeks, one might have said that Cari, or the class, had nearly eliminated Ben's disruptive behavior. However, such an explanation would miss the point, because Ben had eliminated his disruptive behavior. Ben was also beginning to care about other students. He was following the rules. Being successful became important to him. He was still behind other students in readiness for first grade. Even so, one could see that learning was becoming easier for him. By the end of the year he was nearly caught up, and achieved minimum criteria for first grade. Ben's behavior problems in the previous class were not because it was his nature to behave inappropriately. His behavior in the previous class and his behavior in his new class was greatly influenced by the teacher-directed interactions. The students in Cari's class helped Ben, because they were dedicated to the common cause of helping each other excel.

The methods Cari used were important to Ben's success. However, usually by midyear, if not before, one can notice another agent of change that helps students excel. The classroom culture does much of the work. Consider what Ben saw when he came into his new class. He saw every student attentive and comfortable. He did not see anything that suggested a system of warnings or threats. Ben did not see any students in trouble for their behavior. All students were polite and courteous to him and each other. He never heard a student warn him about getting in trouble, and no one told him that certain behaviors were prohibited. Students talked about how they behaved in their class. They helped him understand how he should behave. Only occasionally did Cari explain to him the rationale for classroom behavior. She had taught all students to behave appropriately. Students did not worry about forgetting a rule, because the social approval helped them remember how to behave. In her entire teaching career, she has seldom spent much time intervening to stop inappropriate behavior. In that school year, her methods over the first two months developed a positive classroom culture. The culture was not centered on what behaviors were forbidden; the culture in this class emphasized the proper way to act. By the time Ben arrived, the culture, with some help from Cari, did the work of teaching him how to behave in his new class. Other students did not assume a coercive position of telling him what to do, but instead described what they do. She used methods designed to get her students to help each other become responsible citizens.

Students helping each other is typical when teachers place an emphasis on everyone working together. Once students accept that they have a responsibility to everyone, they learn how to help each other. The teacher's job becomes easier. Even preschool and kindergarten students can unite for a common purpose. They have learned how to act and understand the importance of behaving appropriately. Students at very young ages can follow the rules and discipline their own behavior. Few reminders and almost no consequences will be necessary, and the students will help each other. Once a teacher learns the process, she can bring a new group to this point in just a few weeks. In as little as six weeks, we have seen preschool teachers serving students with severe emotional disorders develop acceptable behavior from every student. The methods make it possible.

Creative Solutions for Problem Behavior

Despite how good their methods are, teachers will encounter some difficult behavior. However, clever teachers can frequently transform a negative situation into a positive outcome. Consider the earlier fundamental — whatever affects one student, also affects other students in the group. Those effects could be positive or negative toward accomplishing the common purpose. Nevertheless, teachers can reduce the negative effect and produce a positive outcome. Let us consider an example and see how it could play out. This example is chosen because over the years

Art has seen similar examples play out differently. Suppose Aviana drops her books and Juan offers to help her pick them up. The offer will affect Aviana. She will most likely feel as though Juan accepted it as an accident and did not fault her for the mishap. She might allow him to help and thank him for his help. Whether the teacher responds or even sees the interaction, there will be a positive effect on those two students and those who saw the encounter. Because Aviana accepted and appreciated the kindness, other students would be more kind in the future.

If, however, Juan kicks her books and calls her clumsy, the effect will be different. Aviana's feelings will be hurt and she might feel bad for the entire day. The effect on Aviana will be magnified because it has happened in front of her peers. Even so, other students can have varying reactions. Some may feel sorry for Aviana, others could admire Juan's courage in being antisocial, and still others will consider him a jerk. Teachers should recognize that being considered clumsy is not beneficial for Aviana, and being considered a jerk will not help Juan.

If a teacher sees the incident, her response will have an impact on the reactions of all students. Consider three examples of how the teacher might respond. She could respond by sending Juan to timeout and have Aviana pick up her books. In this example, other students will see that she does not approve of what Juan did. However, with this response some students may still admire Juan, because that is the way to treat clumsy girls. Others might be happy that Juan was sent to timeout; they may think he got what he deserved. Still others could respond by thinking the teacher is too mean. This response from the teacher could affect the productivity of several students for several minutes.

Consider how it turns out if the teacher responds differently. She might say, "Juan, kicking her books is not helpful. You need to help her pick those up and apologize to her." If he follows her instructions, she has a good start on helping the incident turn positive. Other students will get the message that she is concerned about Aviana and does not approve of Juan kicking her books. The negative effect on Aviana would be at least partially negated. We have known many teachers who will get it right to this point. However, we have also seen teachers let it slip away after Juan picks up the books. Often we have seen teachers who would then turn to Juan and admonish him for kicking the books. The problem with the admonishment is that the teacher failed to appreciate his behavior had changed from unacceptable to acceptable the moment he picked up the books. For the teacher to admonish him then would be a negative inter-action following the appropriate behavior of picking up the books. If a teacher wants him to follow her instructions in the future, a reinforcer must follow his picking up the books. The teacher used an admonish-ment because she thought a punishment was needed for the behavior of kicking the books. If instead, she thanked him for picking up the books, the situation is over and it has a positive outcome. If she feels it is neces-sary, she can talk to Juan about the matter later. However, embarrassing Juan does not help any more than it does if Aviana is embarrassed.

Consider a third possible outcome. The teacher asks Juan to pick up the books and he refuses. These situations may become problematic in classrooms. A teacher may feel the student had challenged her authority. She might think she needs to make him pick up the books immediately. This example usually ends in a power struggle and may have detrimental effects on Juan, other students, and maybe even on the teacher.

However, Tammy Lindner, a fourth grade teacher, handled the situa-tion differently. After Juan kicked the books, she said, "Carrying books can be hard. I know. I have dropped mine a hundred times. When I do, I always appreciate it when someone helps me pick them up. Are there any volunteers to help Aviana?" A dozen hands shot up.

Tammy said, "Look, everyone wants to help. I am so proud. This is an example of good citizenship. Aviana, why don't you choose someone to help you?" Aviana chose Cassie. Tammy did not mention the students who did not volunteer.

Tammy said, "Thank you Cassie for helping Aviana." In this example, Aviana felt special because so many people wanted to help. The students who volunteered to help were made to feel special. Tammy also avoided the possibility anyone would think she played favorites by letting Aviana choose who would help. Juan is about the only one who did not have a chance to be special in the teacher's eyes. However, she did not punish him. She did not reprimand him. She did not embarrass him, but she did talk to him later. Tammy knew that much work needed to be done to help Juan become responsible and self-disciplined. However, his behavior problems would not be solved in a day. She knew it would take weeks or maybe months for him to become the cooperative student she envisioned. What happened on this day was just a tiny part of what she had planned for him. Her actions were mostly intended to prevent other students from imitating Juan. Watching Tammy Lindner teach was a privilege. Over time, Juan became cooperative and all of the students blossomed into wonderful young people. These wonderful young people were part of helping Juan become a cooperative student, and he also helped them.

In a different example, Jerome had permission to go to the restroom. When he came back, he walked past Marco and slugged his shoulder. Marco screamed and jumped out of his seat. Jeannine Bruckner, the fifth grade teacher said in a stern voice, "Boys stop." They stopped and looked at her. She went directly to them to learn what had happened. Nevertheless, solving that issue was only part of what was on her mind. The entire class had quit working and was wondering what was going to happen. When she reached the boys, it might surprise some to learn, her priority was not what had happened between them, but how to get the rest of the students back to work. Eventually, before the school year was half over, she would want such an incident to have little or no influence on how other students continued to work. The time to start on her goal was now. She said to the class, "Everyone, you still have work to do, I will take care of this."

She turned her attention to the boys. When she felt like she had a good handle on what had happened, she complimented Marco for not hitting back. The whole thing, she learned, had started on the playground before school. She talked to Jerome about it not being acceptable to hit others. He had to find a different way to handle his anger. The teacher stopped for a moment and praised several students for returning to work. This was necessary to help other students learn they could continue working and not let distractions cause them to lose valuable time needed to excel in the fourth grade.

Returning her attention to the boys, she finished her discussion with them. The consequence was for both boys to write an apology to each other and to the class for disrupting their work. She explained to Jerome,

"When you get your feelings hurt, you need to handle it peacefully or get the teacher's help. You cannot hit other students." Marco needs to learn to refrain from hurting the feelings of others. The point we want to make is that she needs the students, including these boys, to learn to work through distractions. Even if a teacher were to assume that a consequence would reduce the chances of similar behaviors occurring in the future, she would still have to teach the students how to respond appropriately. However, the consequence, which might have failed, would have made it more difficult for her to teach the appropriate way to behave in school. Jeannine also talked to them about how they had disrupted other students; therefore, they wrote an apology to everyone. She added, "All students have a right to a classroom where achievement is possible. We, as a class, cannot excel if we fight and disrupt others." The class needed to learn to trust her to take care of such issues so they could continue toward their goals. Because this teacher wants her class to excel, she must accept the responsibility of helping these boys.

While this method may have taken a bit more time than a quick consequence, the time was well invested. Jeannine helped the students learn how to handle problems. In just a few short weeks, she had few problem behaviors from students. She had taught students to work through distractions and help each other.

No teacher wants to deal with too many behavior problems. However, problems should not be feared. Teachers can take care of virtually any problem that can arise in their classrooms. Not only can they use their interactive skills to handle any problem that arises, but they can use occasional behavioral problems to strengthen students' commitment to continuing to work no matter what happens. Teachers can also transform problems into positive events. The students individually and as a group will help a teacher create a positive learning experience.

Creating a Positive Culture

Any group will become either productive or nonproductive. A classroom full of students is often considered nothing more than a means for efficiently delivering course material. This is a narrow view of a class. Academic instruction can now be distributed to students individually via the internet. The most significant advantage of schools are classrooms with many students; by taking advantage of group dynamics, teachers can achieve incredible results that are impossible with individual instruction.

Teachers must always be concerned with how they will get the group to function together and become successful. All teachers must understand that the issue is not about what is easy for them and never about a specific incident. To be effective, teachers must understand that the issue is how the class functions as a group. The class must become a functional, not dysfunctional, group. A functional group does not let distractions derail its purpose, but instead becomes dedicated to the goal of learning. We call this a positive culture. Each student works toward their own goals and simultaneously develops a genuine concern for the success of all other students. Each student works for the benefit of everyone, and everyone works toward the benefit of each. They must be as concerned about each other as they are themselves.

A positive culture is developed through the positive use of interactive skills. The authors realize this perspective is about a hundred and eighty degrees different than traditional teacher training. Most teachers have been trained to deal with every incident and not concern themselves with the group as a whole. Unfortunately, that approach limits academic accomplishments for nearly all students in the class. Administrators often expect teachers to deal with every behavioral issue as if it were happening on an island. They endorse and adopt intervention procedures involving warnings, threats, and consequences without an understanding of the broader implications. Before criticizing teachers and administrators, we recommend taking into account that until now these methods have not been readily available. The fundamentals of group dynamics, adverse effects of coercion, and an understanding of the teacher/student relationship are a few of the new concepts included in these methods.

The positive culture creates the energy that propels everyone to excel. Most have heard it said, "A team can become greater than the sum of the parts." So it is with a class, every student becomes a better human being because of his classmates. The culture propels each to excel and every student contributes to the culture.

Every good coach, even of young adults, will know how members develop an emotional alliance with other members of the team. They become emotionally invested in the common cause, but also in the contentment of every fellow team member. The same thing should happen in classrooms. For classrooms to be effective, students must develop constructive relationships with the other students. Teachers are looking for and trying to develop a constructive emotional alliance between students. A good example is the earlier story of Ben. The class did everything a teacher could expect to help him succeed. Additionally, they also came to care about him. A mutual alliance developed between many members of the class and Ben. Because he joined the class in January, he benefited from the culture that was in place. By using the methods described in this book, Cari did not have to devise techniques to stop Ben's problem behavior. Instead, the continuation of the methods she had used all year and the culture that had developed affected a positive change in the way Ben behaved.

In schools, an inordinate amount of time is spent on behavior management. Typically, we see teachers spending between one and three hours per day managing contingency systems. Earlier we explained how a tangible reinforcement system can easily take an hour per day of the teacher's time. However, the management of any system that includes any consequences for inappropriate behavior or warnings for students to change their behavior will result in students finding ways to distract or disrupt class activities. In the worst cases this can consume an additional two hours per day of class time. From the teacher's perspective, this is not what they want to do, but instead is what must be done. Many teachers and administrators assume that if teachers did not spend this amount of time managing behavior, no learning would take place. When teachers learn interactive teaching, the time spent on dealing with inappropriate behavior can, within a few weeks, be reduced to a few minutes per day. After a few days with a new class, the time Cari spends on behavior issues is sometimes only seconds per day. In her classes, after about three weeks with a new group of kindergarten students, the behavioral issues are not a major factor. By midyear, she will sometimes go a whole week without any behavioral issues that require her attention. Every teacher in this country can have that situation in their class.

When teachers attempt to find the appropriate consequence for inappropriate behavior, they have effectively taken responsibility for class behavior away from the students. Consequently, students are no longer responsible for what happens in class. Instead of teaching students to manage their own behavior within the rules, the teacher has assumed the position of notifying students of rule violations. If the problem belongs to the teacher, she must impose the solution. The alternative is to get students to relish the autonomy and responsibility of showing how well they can follow the rules. When powerful positive recognition follows even a small portion of the appropriate behaviors, nearly every student will ascend to trustworthiness.

The authors have heard teachers say many times that we obviously do not know their students. However, the authors have effectively worked with extremely difficult students. Some students will be more difficult than others and a few will be extremely difficult; nevertheless, if the methods are closely followed, all students will respond. The suggestion of needing different procedures with some students misses the point. Because all students are human, the process will be effective. The teacher does not make the inappropriate behavior her problem; instead, her objective is to construct an environment where students can be the solution. With these methods, teachers are not responsible for addressing, or even noticing, every rule violation. With a positive system of social approval, teachers have considerably more room for imperfection. Behaviors become stronger when only some instances are reinforced. Teachers are responsible for creating and reinforcing appropriate behavior. Their job is to use the science of human behavior to encourage productive learning, and to avoid methods that impede learning.

Unfortunately, teachers who are reading this may never have seen the process work. They may feel that they are staking everything on a process they have never used. However, if a teacher praises appropriate behavior twice a minute for three hours, she will see a promising change. Teachers who do this for several weeks usually produce enough change to believe in the methods.

This chapter has illuminated many shortcomings with some standard procedures. However, we hope teachers can see beyond the detrimental procedures, and instead see new methods for helping students excel. For many in this field behavioral issues have become an insurmountable hurdle. Is the solution hidden somewhere out of sight? The answer is no. On the first day when students fill the classroom, the problem and everything necessary for the solution are both present — the students. The mission is to educate a group of students and the group is the solution; therefore, teachers are faced with learning how to get voluntary cooperation from every student. Coercion will complicate, not solve the problem and a teacher's frustration will impede the common purpose. A teacher who tries to chase down every rule violation will not advance the pursuit of academic accomplishments.

Some administrators will say, "It sounds good, but such sweeping changes are not practical." However, nothing could be more practical; the solution is to understand and address the psychological nature of students. Also, many teachers will say, "I just need a way of dealing with the two or three problem students and my class will be okay." No one can create coercive techniques that will stop inappropriate behavior. The interventions are part of the problem, not the solution. Because administrators are busy plugging holes in the dike, they may be reluctant to embrace a new approach to teaching. Nevertheless, that is the only solution. Unless these solutions are implemented, our schools will languish and eventually be replaced with computers. If schools are replaced with computer instruction, we will lose the greatest asset in the education of children — the group.

Question and Answer

Question: From what you say, I apparently have to start over in learning how to teach. That is overwhelming.

Answer: No, most of what you learned in your teacher training program is very valuable. You know a great deal about child development, curriculum, and subject matter that is not affected by anything in this book. Art always prefers to train credentialed teachers. Nevertheless, many individuals with nothing more than a high school education can learn the methods described in this book. With appropriate methods, credentialed teachers can manage conduct behavior and appropriately educate students. Your classroom can be the envy of most teachers. The difference is simply a set of skills that are seldom taught in teacher training programs. You are an intelligent and capable individual and can learn these skills.

Summary of Interventions to Avoid and Why

Contraindicated Interventions	Rationale
Any intervention that focuses on consequences for inappropriate behavior is contraindicated. These would include a stoplight system, happy/sad face chart, taking away privileges, or home notes.	Behavioral research shows that the effectiveness of punitive consequences is questionable. Our experience has revealed unwanted side effects. In classrooms, we have found four typical side effects: (1) a negative effect on teacher/student relationships; (2) negative effects on unification for a common purpose; (3) students being shamed in front of their peers; (4) increased student anxiety that will interfere with learning.
Avoid the routine use of countable reinforcers such as points or a purple card system.	When teachers rely on using reinforcers that can be tallied, it results in some students being identified as less capable. The learning of these students may be adversely affected for the remainder of the year. Also, resentment among students results in adverse effects on the unified purpose.
Teachers should never favor certain students.	When a teacher plays favorites, it affects her relationship with all other students. She becomes less respected as a leader.
Avoid interventions that put the teacher at odds with the students. Criticism or derogatory remarks are examples.	When a teacher is at odds with some students, her credibility as a leader has been compromised. ☞

Contraindicated Interventions	Rationale
Avoid reinforcement systems that require a summary evaluation of behavior over a period.	The skills necessary for any student to become an effective learner must be specifically identified and reinforced immediately following the response.
Teachers cannot allow student behavior to derail positive methods.	If teachers become locked into punitive interventions for inappropriate behavior, students will define the culture of the classroom.

An Effective Interaction Teachers Should Use and Why

Interactions that Benefit Learning	Rationale
Keep students working even when distractions are present.	Students cannot learn if they allow themselves to become distracted. Teachers must work at maintaining student work despite distractions.

8

Dealing with Extreme Behavior

Emotion First, Behavior Second

No MATTER HOW WE DESCRIBE THE PROCESS of creating coopera- tive behavior, some teachers always insist that they have to have methods to deal with very extreme behavior. The truth is they are right. Even if teachers are really good at developing excellent behavior, and never use any coercive methods, the potential of extreme behavior will exist. This chapter will address a few less coercive methods for handling serious behavior.

Art was in a meeting with another teacher when Mrs. Lambert, a new teacher, sent an assistant to have Art come to the classroom at once because Bryan had to be disenrolled. He went in expecting to find chairs and tables turned over, most of the materials thrown off shelves, material torn off walls, and backpacks in every corner of the room. However, that was not so; instead, he found a box of crayons dumped on the floor. The teacher could not understand how anyone could even think that such a child could ever be educated. While this does represent one of the more extreme examples of a teacher overreacting, every administrator has dealt with a similar situation. This teacher, like many others, had little training in how to help every student develop appropriate behavior; therefore, she felt helpless when she encountered problem behavior. She was frustrated because she had often seen times where consequences did not work.

Responding to teachers who resent serious misbehavior, administra- tors sometimes create zero tolerance policies. Many schools are proud of their intolerance for bad behavior and have policies that mandate suspension or assignment to a special class. We have no idea what educators hope to accomplish with a suspension. Apparently, the idea is that if a student were not allowed to attend a school he never wanted to attend in the first place, he would decide to behave himself when he was mandated to return.

In a perfect world, teachers would never be expected to respond to extreme behavior until they had become very accomplished at developing cooperation. Because "perfect" will never exist, administrators need to accept that most teachers will have difficulties with behavior problems. They will make mistakes before they can independently handle every student without any help.

The teacher's complaint led Art to expect one of the worst problems he had ever seen. Instead he found a minor misbehavior to which the teacher had overreacted. This example not only allows us to describe the process, but how a teacher's perception of the problem can be as important as the problem itself. When the teacher complained to Art about having to clean up an entire box of crayons, he responded by saying, "Why would you clean them up?"

She responded, "But I can't leave them there for the rest of the year."

"I'll show you how to do it," he responded. By raising her voice to the boy and threatening to kick him out of school, the teacher had made the problem much worse than a simple box of crayons dumped on the floor. Art walked slowly over to the kindergarten student and sat on the floor beside him. The boy turned away and would not look at him. Without saying a word, he laid his hand gently on the boy's shoulder. The boy did not pull away, so he left his hand there. After a few seconds he said, "Maybe I can help." Several seconds later the boy slightly adjusted his position so that, if he chose, he could see Art. At this point, Art said, "I know it's hard." The words were far less important than the empathy with which they were said. After another several seconds the boy glanced at him and he asked the boy, "Can we talk about what's wrong?" The boy nodded his head. If the boy had not accepted the opportunity to talk, Art would have continued the process until the boy was ready to talk.

Almost invariably, teachers will describe this approach as stupid, because they think empathy would reinforce the behavior. Readers, by this point, should recognize that too much time — more than a few seconds — has passed for the interaction to influence the behavior. The boy was sitting quietly to the side of the room when Art approached him. However, even if the boy were still in the middle of a tantrum, the process would be the same. To deal with the issue, Art had to get the boy to process information through his prefrontal cortex. The boy was in no mood to open his brain to anyone. Art had to get the boy to talk about the issue, but he could not make the boy talk. He had to be patient until the boy was ready. When a student expects to be ridiculed, he will resist cognitive processing of information. This boy had previously learned he could trust Dr. Willans, but he had to be sure that was still the case before he would even look at him. Once he was willing to talk, Art first talked with him about what happened to upset him and then about his behavior. They talked about what the boy could have done differently. Finally, he said to the boy, "We have some crayons to clean up."

We call this process, "Emotion first, behavior second." This label describes how empathy or emotion is the first order of business in responding to many severe behavioral issues. When an emotional component is evident, the "emotion first" process is necessary.

Until a distraught student is calmed down, the only thing that can be done is to express empathy and bring the emotion under control so the child can engage in a rational process. Once teachers accept that punishment, coercion, and shaming are not going to reduce inappropriate behavior, which is even more true when a child is agitated or frightened, the only possibility left is to seek a rational solution. Because the emotional center of the brain, the amygdala, cannot reason, the solution starts with bringing the emotion under control. Having calmed the amygdala, the child could process the information through his prefrontal cortex; he could be reasonable. Often, teachers will complain that such a process will not stop extreme behaviors from ever occurring again, and that is true. However, it is also true that no consequence, except death, can put a permanent stop to severe behavior.

The process would not be any different if the boy had hurt a teacher, thrown a chair, or broken a window. Addressing the behavior is impossible until the child is willing to engage in a cognitive interaction.

Invariably, teachers vigorously object, "You would not use consequences even if a child broke a window?" Our answer is, "You are correct."

Art recalls an instance when a student punched a teacher in the face and broke her nose. The consequences were for him to help clean up the blood, get her another box of tissue, a fresh ice pack, and a wash rag for her face. We are not a court of law; we do not mete out justice. Our objective is to teach students to control their emotions and discipline their behavior. The next day the teacher was back working with the boy. She reinforced his appropriate behavior and helped him with his work. She did not hold a grudge but treated the boy with gentleness, like any other student. This was a breakthrough in his treatment; his violent behavior decreased sharply after that.

Unlike common behavioral issues, extreme behavior is a result of emotional distress. Extreme behavior usually requires an intervention beyond differential social attention before it is resolved. When extreme behavior occurs, the first thing that must be done is to be sure that everyone is safe, which may require a physical intervention. Most schools have protocols for physical interventions. We are not going to address the issue except to say that everyone, including the aggressor, must be kept safe. Once everyone is safe, the teaching intervention is cognitively to engage the student. However, the prefrontal cortex cannot be engaged until emotion is under control.

De-escalation of Emotional Responses

The de-escalation of emotional responses is not a topic many teachers have studied. All humans are emotional and younger children generally have limited ability to regulate their emotions. However, once schools were mandated to serve all students, they had to find ways to help even those with severe emotional disturbances. The typical systems for serving these students have been strict behavioral systems. Applied behavior analysis has not been very effective in rehabilitating students with severe emotional issues. However, commonly the problem was compounded as schools adapted these techniques for classrooms. Despite efforts, trying to adapt contingency systems for severe behavioral and emotional issues offers little hope. The results of studies from a half century ago should have made that conclusion obvious. Since then, research in neuropsychology has eliminated any hope of finding success with coercive methods.

This process of de-escalation is to establish a personal, empathic connection with the student. Connection, not consequences, is the path to correcting behavioral issues. This process is easier when teachers have a strong relationship with all students. In a classroom, every student knows how the teacher treats other students. A teacher who has a good relationship with students and no history of being punitive can slowly and gently help agitated students. The process involves speaking softly and not making demands of the student. Art has sometimes sat on the floor for more than an hour waiting for a student to regain emotional control. Readers should understand that if the student gets out of the area where other students are, supervision must be maintained. The situation with the boy dumping the crayons was also complicated because a teacher had threatened him with serious consequences. If Art had started by demanding the boy talk about the problem, the student may or may not have complied. However, any demands would have solidified the student's contempt for all staff. With emotional dysregulation, the de-escalation process is to use a soft voice, empathic words, and gentle touch. Teachers should be sensitive to variations with some students. Sometimes a gentle touch will help; however, in some instances we would advise the teacher to offer her hand to the student and wait for the student to initiate the touch.

Teachers may object that they cannot spend that much time on one student. Some teachers can manage a group of 25 students and simultaneously give 10 or 15 minutes to helping one student de-escalate. However, other alternatives are available. For instance, if a student were standing on a table and threatening other students, choices still exist that protect students and decrease the chances of further escalation of the problem. Some teachers have taught their students to move to the far side of the classroom, away from the out-of-control student and manage themselves. Sometimes, the teacher could call the office for help. Also, one student could go to the nearest classroom and get help. The second teacher could call the office or have all of the other students come into her classroom.

Even in instances of extreme behavior, such as violence or serious property destruction, teachers have choices. The more extreme the problem, the more important it is for the teachers to de-escalate the emotion before dealing with the behavior. This is an abbreviated version of the necessary steps in the de-escalation of severe emotional distress and preparing teachers to handle the most difficult situations. A complete description of this process would require more chapters. The authors may undertake such a discussion in future writings. However, Art has trained paraprofessionals who have learned the process with little more than the preceding discussion.

We also get concerns that teachers should never touch students. Gentle touching is beneficial in helping students regain emotional regulation. If schools are going to serve students who are emotionally dysregulated — a federal mandate — appropriate touch is therapeutically necessary. Remember, the teacher also has the choice of offering her hand and letting the student initiate the touch. An outstretched hand is a universal sign of offering help. For nearly all students, a touch promotes emotional regulation. However, those students who have been physically mistreated in other settings may not regain emotional control until they are certain that no one will physically harm them. If a teacher knows that history, we would advise an extensive de-escalation before offering one's hand.

Once the student is emotionally ready to discuss his behavior, the process becomes straightforward. The best situation is for the student to be able to describe his behavior and what provoked him. However, if he cannot describe what he did, the teacher must describe the behavior. She will describe what he did and how students need to act.

Teachers must accomplish this reasoning process at the child's developmental level. We have not found this issue to be difficult, especially for experienced teachers. The discussion with the child will focus on what happened and how he felt about what happened. However, within this process is a trap for teachers. While revisiting his thoughts is important for the child, teachers cannot allow the student to make excuses for his behavior. They should get the student to describe what happened and the proper way to behave in the situation. Teachers have heard a thousand times, "But he hit me first." One student hitting another student does not justify retaliation. The student who got hit can either take care of the situation, or get help from a teacher; however, he is not allowed to retaliate. We typically teach students to take care of the problem by using their words. We have heard kindergarten children explain to the offending child, "We do not hit, because we have to keep each other safe." Young children usually think they should be allowed to get even if another student hits or kicks them. If the world followed this logic, fighting would last forever. Teachers will, if necessary, simply explain the rule, "You cannot hit back."

If a student creates a mess, he needs to help clean it up. Many teachers will, however, at this point reignite the emotional outburst. While the logical consequence is for the student to clean up his own mess, nothing is gained unless the teacher can get him to do so without another outburst. Instead of telling the student what he has to do, teachers should use a statement like, "We have a mess to clean up." The best situation is for the student to clean up the entire mess; however, students can make messes that are bigger than they can clean up. Most of the time, teachers will need to direct how to clean up the mess, and may sometimes need to help the student in some way. Teachers must remember, once the student is cleaning up the mess he is behaving appropriately and needs to be reinforced for his work. In fact, the social approval for making things right is an important part of the treatment process.

If a teacher is the only adult in the classroom, and all students are safe, she first attends to getting the rest of the students working independently. Dealing with the problem behavior does not have to be rushed unless the behavior continues. The student will not be ready to talk to the teacher for a few minutes anyway. When the other students are working independently, the teacher goes to the individual student. While she addresses the situation with the student she must also direct some of her attention to keeping the other students working. The teacher will look away about every minute or two and praise those students who are working. This alternating of attention can, if necessary, continue for several minutes. In those situations when it takes much longer, the teacher can simply say to the student, "I'll be back in a little while."

Logical Consequences

In situations where inappropriate behavior occurred, a teacher might want to use a logical consequence. A logical consequence would be one that is closely related to the behavior. For instance, if a student made a mess, having him clean it up would be a logical consequence. However, we have seen many instances where teachers will use logical consequences incorrectly. One mistake in using logical consequences is that they are frequently used as punishment. Perhaps this is partially because it is called a consequence, but imposing it as a punishment will compromise the effectiveness. When Art talked to the boy about the crayons on the floor, he said, "We have a mess to clean up." He did not say, "Now get over there and clean up that mess." This becomes even more important when dealing with students who have severe emotional problems. Had Art imposed a consequence, the boy probably would have stormed off. One might assume he would conclude, "He doesn't care about me. He only cares about the stupid crayons." The boy must trust throughout this process that Art is there to help him learn to deal with the problem he had. He must know that he is important to Art. The student should understand that no one is going to make him pay for his mistake.

Sometimes when a child literally destroys a classroom, the teacher will need to clean up much of the mess. Nevertheless, the student should help as much as possible. We mentioned earlier that when using a logical consequence the teacher cannot hold a grudge. Everything is empathetic or matter of fact until the student is behaving appropriately. The moment the student has started helping, he is behaving appropriately; therefore, the teacher should praise his work. Should a teacher continue to be mad and negative with her comments to the boy, the problem behavior will most likely resurface. If teachers are not adequately trained in behavioral principles, they might assume being pleasant to the boy would reinforce his bad behavior. Because the behavior happened several minutes before, no consequence, positive or negative, can influence the event. Using a punitive consequence a few minutes after the problem occurred would be contrary to the science of human behavior. Instead, the process we describe is intended to calm the emotion and rationally address the behavior that occurred. Aversive consequences do not work very well, and for serious misbehavior will complicate the issue. The teacher must elicit a rational response, not an emotional response, from the student. Remember, the interactive teaching process is designed to teach students to listen, remember, and act according to what they have learned.

Readers will want to know about the crayons that were left on the floor. Teachers who work for Art never have a problem with this. They all know the student will eventually clean up his own mess. They also know that no supervisor will be upset if they come in and find a mess. Even a huge mess should be left until the student can help. All staff know that cleaning up the mess immediately would mean they had put the order of the classroom above the treatment program. For the student to benefit, he must go through a process that includes: (1) empathy from a staff member; (2) description of the appropriate behavior and the rationale for such behavior; (3) the logical consequences for the issue; and (4) praise for responsible behavior. The effectiveness will be compromised if any portion of this process is omitted or used as a punishment.

Depending on the problem behavior, a logical consequence might not be applicable. For instance, if a child ran through the classroom and bumped into another student, a different but related process might be appropriate. A teacher will most likely find it unnecessary to deal with the emotion first. Typically, the teacher could simply say, "David, what is the rule about running in the classroom?" David would answer and the teacher would follow up with a question about why we have that rule. Quite possibly, David would answer correctly. At that point the teacher might ask David to go back and practice walking through the classroom without bumping into anyone. Depending on how often the issue has come up with David, the teacher would adjust the process. She might have him practice walking through the classroom and past other students once or twice. This procedure is called *positive practice* and is designed to get the appropriate behavior to occur, so it can be reinforced. After all, reinforcing the appropriate behavior is the only way to develop it. David would be expected to apologize to the student he bumped.

Another use of positive practice is valuable to teachers. Suppose a teacher asked her students to form an orderly line. When her first graders lined up they did okay, but not as perfectly as she wanted. She wanted them to go back and practice. She does not want to use this as a logical consequence. They did nothing wrong. She uses it as practice. When a basketball player practices his three point shot, it is not necessarily because he has done it wrong. He wants to practice to improve his shot. If teachers send a group back to practice something again, it might be so the students can get better at the activity.

This process can also be used as a positive teaching procedure instead of a logical consequence. Again, teachers should not use the process as punishment. Imposing negative consequences typically results in problems teachers do not anticipate. The more positive a teacher can be, the more positive her students will be. The ultimate purpose in education is to get students to manage their own behavior. To promote that purpose, teachers must transfer the responsibility to students. When teachers impose consequences, they have assumed responsibility for the students behaving appropriately. The process we advocate will be effective with the best and most difficult of students alike. As a few of the students take responsibility for their own behavior, the classroom culture begins to do the work. When students begin behaving appropriately, the teacher will want to celebrate students being responsible. Teachers can celebrate when students are practicing responsible autonomy.

Using Timeouts

Writing about techniques for problem behavior would not be complete without mentioning timeouts. Timeouts are perhaps the most used procedure in schools for inappropriate behavior. The use of timeout procedures has been studied and may sometimes be effective in reducing inappropriate behavior. Timeouts are so named because students are removed from a reinforcing environment. Unfortunately, using a timeout is more complicated than most teachers realize. Four factors must be present for removal from the group to be effective. First, the environment a student is being removed from has to be positively reinforcing for the student. (A teacher should not use a timeout unless the student and other students were receiving teacher approval in the situation.) Second, the environment must continue to be positively reinforcing for other students during the timeout. Third, the student cannot receive any positive reinforcer while he is in timeout. Fourth, the environment must be reinforcing for the student in question when he returns to the group.

All too often these four conditions are not in place when teachers use timeout. Regarding the first condition, the teacher has to have been reinforcing all students, including the offender, immediately before the problem behavior occurred. Most typically, we find teachers use timeouts because they have failed to make the learning environment successful for all students. When a student is frustrated because of his lack of success, he may act out. However, the problem in the classroom could be as simple as a teacher not recognizing a student for his success.

Regarding the second condition, the student cannot receive any attention or reinforcer while in a timeout. The difficulty arises when students find ways of getting attention from the teacher or other students while in timeout. Sometimes, when visiting classrooms we notice that students find it easier to get attention by continuing to act out when in timeout than in class. Some teachers, in attempting to deal with this issue, will make a place for timeout where the student cannot distract other students. An example would be sending a student to the hallway. However, this creates a major disadvantage for the teacher. When a teacher sends a student to the hallway, she cannot see him and he cannot see the success of the other students.

The third requirement is that the environment must continue to be reinforcing for other students while the student is in timeout. The student in timeout must recognize that he is missing the recognition other students are getting. As readers know, because of the need for socialization, total exclusion can motivate students to want to be included. However, we do not recommend total exclusion because teachers can accomplish more by creating a situation where the student sees other students being successful. Having students see the others being successful is a more powerful motivator than being isolated.

When the student goes back into the environment, he must be successful and reinforced for his success. Even one missing condition reduces the probability of a timeout working. When all four of the conditions are present, a timeout for any student is seldom necessary. Even when a timeout is warranted, a student could still sabotage the process by not remaining in his timeout chair. If the student refuses to take a timeout as instructed, the entire procedure is compromised. The success of the procedure has been left in the hands of a misbehaving student. When a student gets up and walks away from a timeout chair, the teacher has very few choices and none of them are good. She could let him walk away, but he could find many things in a classroom to play with or destroy. If she instructs him to return to the timeout chair, she has given him attention during the timeout. The student might find this reinforcing. We are far more concerned about the statement reinforcing the walking away than the original misbehavior.

Often, students can engage teachers in a power struggle over taking a timeout. Teachers should understand, however, that when the classroom is highly reinforcing, students will usually accept a timeout. Because the conditions for not needing timeouts and using timeouts successfully are centered around having a highly reinforcing classroom and using differential social attention, the same conditions can both eliminate the need for timeouts and help teachers use them successfully. While we have some concern that a student being sent to timeout is a bit shaming, the negative effect is greatly reduced if the classroom is a highly reinforcing environment and timeouts are seldom used. One concern is that teachers will often mislead themselves into thinking their classroom is highly reinforcing when that is not true. However, in classrooms where a teacher is creating a very reinforcing environment, she never concerns herself with the question of the effectiveness of a timeout procedure. She most likely will never need to use one. In those instances where she chooses to use a timeout, it will likely work. Even when a timeout does not work, she will have the confidence that other options will be effective. Art has found that if a teacher is using more than a few timeouts a year, her use of interactive teaching is not as good as he expects from teachers.

Perhaps we have ourselves to blame for the next question teachers ask. We encourage teachers to have children practice doing those things they want students to do correctly. As a result, teachers may suggest that they could prevent timeouts from failing by having students practice taking timeouts. We are not advocates of having students practice taking timeouts. Our primary reason is that when teachers have students practice all the required behaviors, they will almost never need to use a timeout.

Even when timeouts might be working, another issue should be considered. Teachers frequently leave students in a timeout past the time of effectiveness. As a result, timeouts can become punitive. We have often heard the advice that the length of a timeout should be one minute for every year of age. This advice is an effort to simplify the procedure for individuals who do not have the skills to recognize when a procedure has reached a point of effectiveness. No child should be left in a timeout longer than is necessary for him to benefit. If teachers want a rule, we would suggest about 30 seconds past the point when the child is quiet.

We have found teachers make another error in respect to the time a student spends in timeout. This mistake is for teachers to make an excuse for leaving the student in timeout. Teachers will complain, "But the student was slouching in the chair." We understand that teachers may want to teach students not to slouch. However, teaching a student to sit up straight cannot be done by ignoring the student while he is slouching. The excuse is, therefore, a flimsy effort to justify not re-engaging with the student.

Using Reprimands Properly

Many teachers use a reprimand for addressing difficult behavior. When used both sparingly and correctly, reprimands can be effective. However, many teachers make the mistake of using reprimands when they are upset with a student. This usually means the reprimand is loud, spoken in a cross tone, and given in front of peers. This will impede getting students to help each other. Students who have been reprimanded in front of their peers will lose trust in the teacher. Without trust the relationship is compromised and teachers must repair it to maximize learning. Losing the trust of one student affects every student. By using loud reprimands or a cross tone, teachers are very likely to trigger anger or anxiety in students, which will not promote better learning. The use of loud reprimands will adversely affect all students.

Teachers can find themselves using reprimands too often, because loud reprimands are very good at stopping misbehavior. Teachers must understand that interrupting unwanted behavior does not decrease its frequency. Teachers must be careful and not allow themselves to become so concerned about the immediate situation that they ignore the future.

When reprimands are used correctly, the inappropriate behavior will usually be reduced. Reprimands are more effective when spoken softly and given in private. When a teacher has a good relationship with every student, it is surprising how much she can accomplish by simply describing what she does not like about the student's behavior. The intervention should always end on a positive note. For instance, a teacher can end such a discussion with a statement about how she is sure the student will do better.

Following is an example where a teacher, Kevin MacDonald, was very disappointed in a student's behavior. The boy, Greg, a third grader, had just torn up a girl's paper. Kevin took him by the hand and said quietly but sternly, "We do not destroy someone else's papers. I am disappointed in your behavior." Greg broke into tears. He felt terrible because he had disappointed Mr. MacDonald. The teacher waited about a minute without saying anything to the boy. Finally, the boy stopped crying. (Teachers should understand, Kevin expressed his disappointment and the boy was ashamed of his behavior, but the teacher did not make a mistake. He did not set out to shame the student.)

After a short discussion of the behavior, Kevin said, "You need to apologize to Danielle." Greg apologized. The teacher suggested he help her redo her paper. Danielle did not want his help because he might not do it right. Kevin had him help her with something else. Danielle said he could sharpen her pencil. This consequence was minor, but the quiet reprimand was effective. A sharp reprimand, accompanied by a consequence, would have triggered Greg to protect himself from the psychological pain. To protect himself he would have made Kevin the enemy. Because the teacher-student alliance was intact, the boy's behavior improved.

Nevertheless, teachers will find situations where a loud reprimand is warranted. In extreme situations, a loud reprimand will stop inappropriate behavior. The appropriate use would be for a teacher to respond loudly to extreme behavior and then instantly change to a different tone. For instance, if several students were picking on another student, a teacher might want to say, loudly, "Stop." The moment the loud command interrupted the behavior, she would change her voice. Sometimes, with an individual student this could be an instant change to a normal tone of voice. In other instances, like the example that follows, the teacher may respond loudly to the behavior of a group and then quickly change to a commanding voice.

This example took place in a classroom where half the students had serious aggression problems. A male teacher had lost complete control of the group and 20 students were in total chaos. Not one student was behaving appropriately. This class was behaving like a mob. Some students were fighting, and others were destroying the classroom. Jana, the teacher from earlier examples, had stepped out of the class where she was serving as a peer trainer for another teacher and noticed the chaos. She rushed into the classroom and shouted in a loud but controlled voice, "Everyone freeze!" The classroom immediately became silent. By raising her voice she bought herself a few seconds to gain control of the class. With complete authority she said, "Everyone over here, on the carpet." The students started moving toward the carpet. She immediately began by telling particular students where to sit. She also began praising students for their compliance and mixed in directions for walking directly, remaining quiet, and keeping hands to themselves. In less than 30 seconds, she had all 20 of the students sitting on the carpet in front of her. Her ability to take charge of the situation was important, but the fact she had established compliance during the previous weeks, when she was temporarily assigned to that class as a peer trainer, was also important. She knew the loud instruction for everyone to freeze would only quiet the group for a few seconds. To get control of the group, she would need to give further instructions and reinforce students who followed those instructions. Many teachers would argue that the students needed to be punished for their atrocious behavior. Any punishment procedure would have triggered emotional distress, especially in those who had an emotional disorder. The first issue had to be to stop the mob behavior before more violence occurred. Once she established order, the use of punishment was out of the question. Even to those who believe punishment was warranted, it cannot follow compliant behavior.

Despite how much Jana might have hoped the students were long past such destructive behavior, much work, which would extend for several weeks, still had to be done. Once the students were quietly seated in front of her, she started a discussion of appropriate classroom behavior and stated her expectation for every student to take accountability for their part in what happened. She expected each student to describe the appropriate way to respond if any such thing were ever to happen again. The students discussed the rules, rationales for the rules, and how they needed to behave. For every student, the lesson was that they could not justify their behavior because of how other students behaved.

Following the discussion, she required the students to clean up the mess. Although they were required to clean up, it was not treated as a punishment. She reinforced the students for cleaning up the mess. We included an extreme example to show how a teacher can be very firm while not being punitive or losing control herself.

Classrooms for Students with Extreme Behavior Disorders

Some students can be very difficult in school. As presented in earlier chapters, the assumption is that because students are going to misbehave, which they will, consequences for such behavior must be available. Nevertheless, punitive consequences are not very effective. Many will assume that because punitive consequences are used in homes and are at least sometimes effective there, this proves their value. While they may be effective for a parent, if used sparingly, where a relationship has existed for years, this does not justify using them in group situations. Also, the use of punitive consequences in schools is ill advised because of the adverse effects on academic accomplishments. Educators are fully aware that permissive parenting is not effective, and they are correct. However, even though the complete opposite of coercive parenting is ineffective, this is not a valid argument for punishing students in school. Teachers can be much more effective using positive procedures to develop appropriate behavior, Despite how many people tell teachers to do it differently, building appropriate behavior is always the most effective process. However, accepting this advice requires both a shift in thinking about how to create appropriate behavior and an understanding of how students respond differently in groups than in family situations.

Sometimes the use of coercive procedures will, on the surface, appear effective in controlling behavior with young children. Before the age of about three and a half, adults can easily coerce children to alter their behavior. Nevertheless, such coercion is not effective treatment for behavioral problems. Even if the behavior can be suppressed for several months, it will reemerge. When the behavior resurfaces, the problem will be more difficult to control. For anyone dedicated to helping children manage their own behavior, the use of coercion is contraindicated. The alternative is to find effective ways to get students to discipline their own behavior.

All the advice in the world does not change the fact that schools must use the teachers they have to educate some very difficult students. Our opinion is that the most difficult students are best and more easily served when integrated into regular programs. When the methods we recommend are correctly carried out, typical students become valuable role models for difficult students. Art was first involved with training elementary teachers to effectively mainstream difficult students more than 40 years ago. His advice to schools begins with identifying those teachers who can effectively work with problem behavior and provide the necessary training. However, we fear that some schools, at least during a transition phase, will find it necessary to continue specialized classrooms for those students with the most severe behavior disorders. Specialized classrooms are not ideal, but Art has been involved with some that were effective with students.

The most notable example will be described here. We will describe a program in a school located in a very violent area of a large city. The students saw violence in the streets several times per week. A frequent conversation among students was about the most recent person that had been shot. Although she was not using interactive teaching exactly, Miss Walsh was using several techniques consistent with it. This example, from a classroom of sixth graders with severe behavior disorders, is worth including in these pages. Of the twelve students, nine were boys. Judy Walsh used differential social attention as her primary motivation device. Nowhere was there any semblance of a punishment system. She did use logical consequences, timeouts, reprimands, and separation from the group as consequences. She frequently had a student teacher, but the school did not give her an aide. Judy did have a direct intercom to the office and if behavior got out of hand she could call for help. She rarely used this and only when she needed a student removed from her classroom for a few minutes until she could bring the rest of the students under control.

The first thing an observer would have noticed was her demeanor. Judy never got ruffled or became upset. However, no student would have failed to notice that she was in charge. No student ever mistook her for mean, unfair, or uncaring about them or their lives. Her attitude was that these students had developed their behavior problems over several years; it would be unrealistic to think she could change them in a day, a week, or even a month. The students knew exactly what she expected of them and why. She never became angry with a student. Her first order of business every year and with every new student was to teach them never to be violent. No observer would have needed more than one glance at the students to concur that her first order of business was a wise decision. Some educators would be surprised to know that teaching non-violence need not involve threats of punishment, or promises of rewards. She helped the students build friendships with each other and come to understand that they were all in this class to stay. She helped each student develop both short- and long-term goals. Some of these goals were related to the school year and some were for their adult life. This might have been considered absurd, since for many of these students a long-term goal of staying alive for the rest of the week was optimistic. Because the concept of "long-term" was itself foreign to some students, she helped them with long-term goals. They were allowed and even encouraged to change their goals. Some goals were unrealistic, but the students never heard that from Miss Walsh. Each day started with the students proclaiming their long-term goal.

When hearing this story, many teachers have said, "But my students could not even remember a goal until the next day." Of course not,

Judy would have said. "We write them down." Most of the words were misspelled, and the sentences were not complete. Misspelled words and poor sentences were okay, because they became the reason to learn to write and spell. She used the long-term goals as the rationales for most of the academic lessons.

Judy explained that she would not give up on them and they were not allowed to give up on themselves or their classmates. Students also learned they had only three ways out of the class. First, when they were promoted to junior high they would no longer be in her class. Of the two remaining alternatives, one way out was to be successful in this class and be moved back to a mainstreamed classroom. The second, was to get sent to juvenile hall. Sometimes staying out of juvenile hall became a rationale for behaving appropriately. Judy used staying out of juvenile hall as a reason for their controlling their own behavior. The first time Art heard her explain this he thought she was going to use a threat of sending students to juvenile hall. However, she never suggested their behavior in school would get them sent to juvenile hall. However, several times every year the students would hear about a time when she had become very sad because one of her students had been sent to juvenile hall. She discussed with the students how violent and aggressive reactions would not help them get along with their classmates. She helped them understand that getting along with those they lived with was important to success in life and staying out of jail. Some students had a parent in jail, and they all knew someone in jail, prison, or juvenile hall. That allowed for discussion on how people go to jail. Some students thought it was because the person got caught. Of course, they were right, but that was not the whole story. However, from the class discussion most concluded the way to stay out of jail was to "always do right." She had them discuss what the worst thing would be about being in jail. Some answers included the food or the lack of freedom. The students were good in these discussions, because they had firsthand knowledge. Many of them had visited someone in jail.

Each year, after just a few weeks, pushing, shoving, and hitting occurred only rarely. Many other unwanted behaviors would continue through much of the first semester. Once, several students in the class, joined in and loudly concocted a story about the teacher's sexual behavior. A visitor heard the whole thing; the story may have been to get his attention. Neither Judy nor the visitor were fazed for a moment. She continued teaching those students who were not taking part in the story. In fact, she slightly adjusted the lesson so that those students who participated in the lesson were having fun and getting lots of attention for knowing the answers. Unable to rile the teacher or visitor, the students gave up the disgusting story in about three minutes. These students never got any reaction from Judy. A few days later she had the students work together on creating a wholesome fictional story to which every student contributed. They chose to make the story about a teacher who had a wonderful family.

She could have successfully stopped the disgusting story and, in the short term, her response would have appeared to work. However, any intervention would have increased the chances of a similar situation in the future. By responding incorrectly, even once, she would have made it more difficult to eliminate the problem behavior. The students would have learned how to upset her and what they had to do to take control of the class. Once a teacher allows student misbehavior to cause her to exert coercive control, the problem becomes more difficult.

During the school year these students worked together to help each other move toward their short- and long-term goals. Every student's goal was eventually written and punctuated correctly. Some students had revised their goals several times. Nevertheless, every student knew his goals by heart. A few of the students had graduated to a mainstreamed class and a few new students had been included. In the end, it was a successful year and every student had moved closer to reaching their goal of being successful as adults.

Question and Answer

Question: In your discussion of emotion first and behavior second, it seems that you expect teachers to have a nonfunctioning amygdala. Teachers are people too. How is a teacher supposed to have a student destroy her classroom, attack her physically, or disrupt everything she is trying to do without becoming upset?

Answer: What a wonderful question. Extraordinary emotional regulation is an excellent attribute for teachers. However, college students pursuing a profession in teaching are not screened for their emotional regulation. Teachers are who they are. When hiring teachers, Art describes emotional regulation as an important attribute. He has found that many teachers, following discussions about the importance of emotional regulation, can improve this aspect of themselves. Administrators can use teachers in ways that allow them to be most successful. An administrator would not be advised to replace Judy with a volatile teacher. We have also found that using groups to train teachers can be beneficial. Teachers can learn from each other to become more controlled in their response to difficult behavior. However, the most important issue in helping teachers is to equip them with the skills and methods to handle every issue. Once teachers have been equipped with effective techniques, they generally develop the ability to control their emotional responses. Administrators should expect teachers who are not equipped with effective techniques to become frustrated. We hope you develop the skills that allow you to be confident in helping students learn to control themselves.

Summary

- Dealing with behavior issues requires teachers to understand that until a student has regained emotional control, he cannot cognitively process the appropriate behavior.
- Teachers can get trapped into using reprimands because the behavior will be interrupted, but it will not decrease in frequency.
- Teachers will find it necessary to take charge and stop dangerous behavior or instances of several students behaving inappropriately. Success with students is dependent on the interactions used.

Effective Interactions Teachers Should Use and Why

What Teachers Need to Do	Rationale
Deal with the emotion first and the behavior second.	Students cannot make better choices unless they process the idea cognitively.
Use an empathic connection to de-escalate emotional students.	When a child is in an escalated emotional state, they cannot cognitively process information.
Discuss the behavior, what provoked the behavior, what the child should have done, and the rationale.	Students cannot make better choices until they thoroughly understand how they should behave and the rationale for such behavior.
Use logical consequences after students understand how they should behave.	Logical consequences are more effective than punitive consequences.
Teachers can use timeouts when all the conditions are present for an effective timeout.	This is an appropriate technique in limited circumstances.

Interactions Teachers Should Avoid Using and Why

Things Teachers Should Not Do	Rationale
Do not exaggerate problem behavior. Describe behavior exactly as it is.	To make progress with students the behavior must be described precisely.
Do not use negative consequences for inappropriate behavior.	Teachers do not want to trigger an even worse emotional reaction by stimulating the amygdala.
When explaining how a student should behave, or when a soft reprimand may be necessary, do not use an admonishment.	Most likely the amygdala is controlling the student's brain following the problem behavior. An admonishment will make things worse.
Do not clean up the mess a child leaves.	Having the child clean up the mess gets the child responding appropriately. The appropriate behavior can be reinforced. This is a necessary step in the treatment process.

9
Implementation and Training

NEARLY ALL EDUCATORS ARE UNDER CONSIDERABLE PRESSURE to get better achievement scores from students. The logic for using pressure to get teachers to produce better academic results would suggest that teachers do not care and that administrators must convince them of the importance. Our experience is that teachers do care, and the chain of pressure puts them in a terrible position. They want their students to succeed. They are using the recommended methods; nevertheless, too many students fail to reach the expected academic level. Teachers are using methods designed to reduce problem behavior, but many students do not respond. Teachers are left to conclude that the students are the problem. Once they have blamed students, they cannot succeed until they recognize that success in teaching is determined, not by students, but by the process teachers use. Unfortunately, administrators often conclude that teachers, not students, are the ones falling short. Establishing universal success in education cannot be attained by pressuring teachers to succeed. Too often the methods provided by administrators are the same ineffective methods they used when they were teaching. However, the task of administrators is not perfectly easy either. Administrators may have opportunities to observe classrooms that are succeeding only because they serve students who would succeed regardless of the methods. They seldom have opportunities to watch students who are succeeding only because of the teaching methods being used.

In our view, this puts both principals and teachers in a difficult position. The demands should never be on accomplishing particular results.

Instead, expectations must be placed on teachers to use a process that produces the desired results. Cari has at times been under much pressure from administrators to do things that are useless in helping students thrive, and sometimes those requirements make her job more difficult. Nevertheless, she is always confident the expected academic and behavioral goals are attainable. However, if, hypothetically, someone forbade her to use the methods described in this book, she could not achieve those goals. Most student failure results from incorrect methods used in schools. While some students will be successful despite these methods, universal success depends on methodology. In his program, Art always puts the pressure on teachers to use the methods described in this book, because he knows that any shortcomings result from how the methodology is applied. Sometimes the teacher does not use the methods correctly; however, at other times he finds that he failed to help teachers adjust the methods perfectly for the problem they were facing. Nevertheless, for 25 years, with the most difficult students, the methods have never been the problem. The pressure should always be to use the methods, and trust that they will produce the change.

Unfortunately, understanding the correct methods is not as easy as one might think. For instance, a principal we know, Stephanie Harper, had been a successful teacher in a suburban school in a state neighboring Nevada. With a healthy desire for advancement, she pursued her administrator credentials and accepted a position as principal in a Title 1 school. She was excited and driven to work hard and no one would have doubted her commitment to the success of her teachers and students. Stephanie tirelessly imparted techniques she had successfully used in her own classes. However, no matter how hard teachers tried to use her techniques, students showed little progress. After three years of working extremely hard, academic achievement scores had only edged up a little bit. Some teachers in the school had moderate success; however, the one teacher who was using interactive teaching had considerable success. Those teachers who were having moderate success did not have a framework to adequately define the process that led to their students' success. The successful teacher was on occasion asked what she was doing, but never given more than a minute to describe her process. This teacher's view was that the principal saw her success as inexplicable. We do not know that this teacher had the necessary skills to train other teachers, but we do know that she knew how to teach. We are left to conclude that the principal did not know how to tap the knowledge of her most successful teacher.

Until now, the teaching methods necessary to accomplish results similar to those we described in Chapter One have not been well defined. In our experience, some principals and administrators have excellent ideas regarding many aspects of teaching, but do not know how to develop superior learners. Unfortunately, how to free children's brains from the stress that prevents learning is not commonly understood; therefore, many principals place considerable pressure on teachers to accomplish impossible goals. Little do they realize that many traditional techniques are not only inconsistent with the fundamentals of groups but also contradictory to the science, neuroscience, and psychological factors of human behavior; therefore, many educators do not have the proper training for developing effective learners. The entire problem facing education is further complicated because the training of interactive skills is not well understood.

One may ask why teachers are not highly trained in all the necessary methods as part of their certification. We caution readers against instant anger at universities that are doing a fine job of preparing teachers in the necessary knowledge. However, because these concepts are new, universities are not doing as well in teaching interactive skills. This issue is complicated, because to teach the necessary skills, universities would need laboratory settings, and such facilities are rare in universities. Despite the complicating factors for universities, school districts have the necessary laboratories — classrooms — to train teachers in interactive skills.

Some teachers feel that learning a new way of interacting with students is overwhelming. However, we would advise readers to remember the example from Chapter Three about a young teacher who, without any specialized training, taught herself an interactive process that was similar to what we teach. Her students achieved exceptional results. We think that with our training she would modestly change her interactions. Nevertheless, she was doing very well with her version and any administrator would be delighted with her results. However, changing to interactive teaching or a similar process does not matter unless the change results in remarkable strides in academic learning. The results we describe are possible in every classroom in every district, but only if teachers use these noncoercive methods correctly.

The excuses for failure have become systemic, creating a barrier to improving education. If too many students are failing to reach grade level criteria, there is only one conclusion: something is wrong with the methods or the application of the methods. Any excuse is just that — an excuse. We are aware that many schools are not blessed with ideal conditions. Parents might not be involved, students may have serious behavioral issues, and the physical plant may be substandard; nevertheless, even these schools can attain exceptional results. When the methods we describe are replicated, nearly every student will achieve to grade level standards or above. Teachers and administrators should commit to methods that produce success for every student. While some individual teachers can possibly train themselves, administrators should anticipate that many teachers are going to require specialized training to master the methods we advocate.

An easy step available to teachers is to read and discuss this book with colleagues. Reading and discussing this material will help teachers: (1) develop an appreciation for a classroom environment that builds self-confidence; (2) develop a determination to succeed; (3) help students autonomously choose a constructive course of action; and (4) free students from fear of psychological pain. Many teachers who appreciate the value of such an environment can begin to structure their classrooms and adjust their interactions to more closely resemble the ideal conditions for the development of young brains. Also, teachers can learn to use their classroom interactions to create an ideal learning environment. By specifically strengthening the necessary behaviors, teachers can have students who become cooperative, listen attentively, remember what they have learned, become self-confident in their ability to learn, and are supportive of how their classmates are learning. When teachers know how to use their interactions to create these attributes, their students will excel. However, our experience has been that many teachers are going to need administrative help to learn new methods of interacting with students.

Also, administrators themselves may need some preparation before they can help teachers. Several years ago Art got a call from a teacher who had worked for him a few years earlier. As they caught up on what each had been doing for the last few years, he found that she was teaching second grade in a medium-sized city in another state. Penny Cameron was in her fifth year of teaching in the district. Each of her first four years in a low-income school, her students had scored very well on end-of-year achievement tests. In fact, in each year, her students had scored better than any other class in the school. She was encouraged after the last school year because her principal and a district administrator had finally recognized her success. Early in her fifth year, in the same school, three district administrators had come to observe her teaching. She assumed they were finally aware of her success and wanted to see her methods. She had been hopeful and confident when they visited and assumed they would notice the methods. When a few weeks later she had not heard anything, she asked about the observation. Penny was told that while she had done well, they had found nothing remarkable about her teaching. They explained that nothing in her teaching accounted for her success. She had hoped that the administrators would notice the methods she was using, but became discouraged when that did not happen. Art believed her when she said that she would have liked the recognition, but more importantly she had hoped that administrators would begin promoting the methods so more students could benefit. Penny asked if she were doing something wrong that made the methods hard to recognize.

Mrs. Cameron said, "I think they were hoping I had found a better way to explain math to the students. If I had set the entire second grade curriculum to music, they would have declared that the reason for the students' success."

Art joked by saying, "Haven't you created a tap dance to entertain students following every reading assignment?" (In her youth, she had once been an accomplished amateur tap dancer.) She laughed, but the joke did nothing to eliminate her discouragement. She had called Art because she was seriously considering leaving the field of teaching following the current year. Penny still loved teaching as much as ever, but felt discouraged because many educators were apparently incapable of understanding how to help students learn. During the conversation she said, "I accept that I am no better than other teachers at teaching reading or math. But I'm good at getting students to learn. The process is the same as we used a long time ago with preschool students."

She and Art assumed the observers were so focused on how she explained lessons that they failed to notice how students were working. They never noticed how she interacted with students. The observers apparently did not understand how well the students could listen to her or concentrate during seatwork assignments. They did not notice that the students could remember better than most other second grade students. Penny wished they had talked to the students and realized how enthusiastic the students were about learning. She also complained, "They didn't recognize the students' ability to discipline themselves and focus on the lessons." Art added, "They did not stay long enough to see that certain types of interactions were totally absent from your classroom and did not understand how coercive interactions destroy learning."

The authors are convinced that the use of coercion is embedded in our schools. For example, Cari has had several visitors who, after watching her class for a few minutes, would notice how every kindergarten student was in their seats and continuously working. The students were not fidgeting, looking around the room, or talking to other students. The work-related behavior looked more like a good class of third graders than kindergarten students. Several such visitors have commented about how strict she is with her students. We think they choose the word *strict* because the only way they can imagine students working like hers do is through coercion. However, coercive methods will not create such excellent behavior. Her response is usually something like, "That is the behavior I get, because that is the behavior I reinforce." Unfortunately, she often feels that the visitors leave having no understanding of what she was saying. Perhaps the issue is hard for most teachers to understand because when they use delayed reinforcers, students cannot learn to continue working. Teachers Art has trained frequently ask about how to better explain their teaching process. Unfortunately, the answer is not an easy one, because to understand the interactive teaching process, one must better understand the behavioral science, group dynamics, neuropsychology, the exact reinforcement process, and the effects of coercion. Most often other teachers and principals are patient enough to listen for a minute or two. Even with extensive preparation describing these methods takes an hour or two.

We think the word *strict* infers the teacher made the students behave that way, and would not tolerate a student being out of his seat. A teacher cannot make two dozen students behave perfectly for more than a few minutes at a time. However, if a teacher approaches the issue from the position of motivating students to stay in their seats and continuously work, students willingly choose that behavior. Prying loose coercion's stranglehold might be impossible; however, coercion will dissolve once teachers see what can be accomplished with interactive teaching.

These stories illustrate the point that administrators must not only observe classrooms but be able to understand the influence of the teacher's interactions. One issue that could affect how well students are learning might be how the teacher explains the lessons. We have no criticism of educators looking at that variable. However, at least in more recent years, we have found more teachers competent in teaching reading, writing, math, social science, and science. When administrators find that they cannot explain a teacher's success, they must look deeper. Observers in Penny's classroom may not have seen what they expected to see, but should have known that something besides chance was responsible for the students' success. While, the administrators may have recognized excellent behavior, they apparently did not recognize the reason for the students' conduct. If student behavior is a problem, or not a problem, observers must determine why. The single most important variable regarding student behavior is the interactive methodology the teacher uses. Frequently, the typical systems for addressing problem behavior are coercive and therefore contraindicated. Also, many schools have blamed their lack of success on how parents are raising their children. We are well aware that parenting has slipped in the last few decades. However, students can and will learn how to behave in school depending on the methods used in their school. When teachers use the right methods, they can reduce or nearly eliminate behavior problems in their classrooms. Teachers confronted with problem behavior seldom understand that the process they are using contributes to those problems. When this is the case, administrators have no choice except to reexamine the process recommended to teachers. The correct use of our methods is not guaranteed by just reading this book. Like anything else, learning the process will take work; nevertheless, every teacher can learn all of the skills we describe.

In those instances where students are disrupting the learning process the administrator must conduct observations and possibly interview students to find the reason. They may find the problem to be any one, or a combination, of several issues. First they must determine if the teacher has made her expectations perfectly clear to students and explained the rationale for those expectations. Often the problem is that while the teacher stated the rules, she did not emphasize them enough for students to learn them. To determine whether or not this is the issue may require the administrator to interview students about the rules and expectations in the classroom. A second problem may be that while the students know the rules, the teacher is not adequately reinforcing the related behaviors. If the problem continues even though the rules are understood and the appropriate behavior is being reinforced there is a near certainty that the trouble is in how the teacher responds when she notices inappropriate behavior. Many times Art has found that teachers will be praising appropriate behavior but continue to direct their attention to minor inappropriate behavior. They may do this through a system of consequences or warnings such as a stop light system or by frequently redirecting the misbehaving student. The use of frequent redirection will usually be enough attention to maintain inappropriate behavior.

Sometimes the students are behaving reasonably well, but are still not learning enough to make adequate progress by the end of the year. When this is the problem, the administrator will want to find the answer to three questions. First, are students listening and remembering what the teacher taught? The administrator will have to find the right opportunities to observe to get the answer, although the problem could be that the teacher is not providing students enough opportunities to practice listening and remembering. A second problem could be the teacher is not providing students enough opportunities to engage in correct responses. These could be verbal or written responses, although at all grade levels seatwork will be necessary so that students can generate responses simultaneously. If the teacher is using enough seatwork, then the question becomes whether students are working constantly. With adequate social reinforcers distributed equally to all students while they attend to their seatwork assignment, students will quickly develop the necessary on-task performance. Very rarely will administrators find instances where seatwork assignments are so poorly designed that learning is hampered. Another problem that administrators will often find is that teachers are wasting so much time that the necessary learning is impossible. When that is the case, teachers usually need considerable feedback before they learn to use their time efficiently.

Many districts have sufficient staff at the school or administrative level to help train teachers. However, administrators may require specific techniques for observing and training interactive skills. Mastering skills is different from learning information. To adopt new skills, teachers must practice those skills. Just like hitting a baseball requires considerable practice, so too mastering all the skills recommended in this book. With practice teachers can become accomplished and comfortable with any of the skills described in the preceding pages. Nevertheless, some teachers should expect that proficiency in these methods will require someone to observe and provide feedback as to their use of the skills. Fortunately, administrators can easily learn to conduct observations and provide feedback.

We recommend that schools begin by only training those teachers who volunteer to become trained in these methods. Requiring teachers to master techniques they do not believe in will almost invariably prove ineffective. Unwilling teachers can find dozens of ways to sabotage the methods. However, we see nothing wrong in gently persuading teachers to learn the skills. Also, Art has, for 25 years, described the methods to every teacher who was applying for a job with his school. He offered positions to those who expressed enthusiasm for the methods.

A criterion that Art has used is for a teacher to demonstrate for 10 to 20 minutes at a time a praise rate of two per minute. Sometimes teachers will need to use a higher rate of praise. However, if they have often shown their ability to use two praises per minute, they can usually recognize and adjust to specific situations. Without specific data from an independent observer, though, many teachers will think they are praising more than they are.

For an observational system to be useful in schools, the system must be manageable within reasonable parameters. Most school administrators have little experience in collecting observational data. Also, schools will have only a limited amount of time to train teachers. Nevertheless, many teachers will become capable despite limited training. Fortunately, many teachers can make considerable progress in mastering the methods with just one or two 20-minute observations a week for a few weeks. The observations must generate two types of information. We suggest constructing observation forms to help in generating consistent information. One part of the observation would be to count the number of positive verbal interactions that will benefit students trying to excel. Part of the form would need to include a small chart that provides space for recording the number of praises per minute and the percent of students on-task at the end of each minute. Observers will need to record such data for several minutes during every observation. The second part of the form is for the observer to make subjective notes on how well the teacher is doing in creating a culture where every student can excel.

Praise statements that are nonspecific in nature should not be counted. For positive interactions to be of much value in creating a positive culture, they must be directed toward individual students, specify the behavior that will benefit the student, and immediately follow that behavior. However, teachers must also learn to distribute their praise equally to all students and across time. To determine if verbal reinforcers are appropriately distributed will require careful observation. To be perfectly accurate or to generate research-level data would be extremely time consuming and impractical for training purposes. Most often, schools can adequately train teachers in the time available. By conducting 10- to 20-minute observations, administrators can see the distribution of praise across time. Also, conducting observations at different times during the day will help teachers remember to distribute praise throughout the day.

Distributing praise equally to all students is also imperative to creating a positive learning environment. However, as described in Chapter Four, a typical mistake is for teachers to only praise a few students. Unfortunately, many observers will also find this mistake hard to detect. Observers who know all the students can make a seating chart by name and track the distribution of praise to all students. However, this becomes difficult to track when the observer does not know all the students. Fortunately, Art has found that the students' behavior will reveal the problem, but helping teachers overcome the problem requires much work. If major behavior problems continue to occur even though the praise rate is high, the problem is usually the distribution of praise. Also, minor behavior problems continuing from a few students may alert the observer to the same problem.

Observers must also keep a close eye on verbal reinforcers being directed to both deportment-type and academic behavior. For instance a teacher could create very good behavior in her class, but achievement results at the end of the quarter might show only marginal improvement. Observers will need to notice the problem and write notes to help the teacher recognize the shortcoming. Art has found that most observers can notice this problem and teachers who have learned half the methods will not resist learning the rest of it.

Through her relationship with students, creation of success, approval of appropriate behavior, and elimination of coercion, a teacher can prepare every student to learn. The teacher can have her class take responsibility for themselves and be willing to help their classmates. Whether it takes a teacher a few weeks or several months to learn the methodology is nearly irrelevant. In subsequent years, she can get her class to the critical point in much less time. She can, for years to come, ensure that every student in her classes will succeed.

Teachers who adopt interactive teaching will apply it differently, and that is okay. We have often observed the best practitioners of these techniques are unique in their application. We would be suspicious of a replication that tried to make every teacher a replica of each other. The use of interactive teaching techniques is not a precise application of the techniques so much as a methodology committed to helping students become purposeful learners and satisfy their psychological needs. For instance, Art would characterize one outstanding teacher he has trained as having remarkable relationships with students. Even young children would go to the end of the earth for her. Another is a master in applying the techniques, and a third has an incredible determination never to let a child fail. These teachers are excellent at all of the principles and techniques of interactive teaching and careful observation reveals many similarities. Nevertheless, variations in how they teach sets them apart from their colleagues who use the same methods.

A principal who wants, over time, to get more teachers to adopt interactive teaching will be glad to know the second group in the same school will find the transition easier. Acquisition of these skills is easier when one can see it practiced in another classroom. Because teachers more quickly gain the necessary skills when encouraged by those already using them, principals should establish opportunities for teachers to benefit from each other's progress.

Some trainers will adopt a style of dropping by a classroom and watching until the teacher makes a mistake. They then interrupt and point out the mistake. Teachers will universally hate this feedback and will soon abandon the new methods. Observation at random times is a good idea; however, the trainer will need to help each teacher build more of the desired methodology. Feedback must concentrate on what the teacher is doing right and how the methods are helping students. Later, perhaps in private, the trainer will want to point out a mistake or two and the rationale for avoiding certain tactics. However, we often get teachers gladly to accept such feedback in a small group of teachers who are learning to adopt the new methodology. If teachers will accept the feedback in this manner, all teachers can benefit from the feedback provided to other teachers.

Review of Methods

We feel an obligation to review how our methods influence students. Students, indeed all humans, pursue their psychological needs throughout their daily lives. When these needs are largely satisfied, students are better able to delay gratification of needs, and to inhibit responses that are contrary to classroom rules. Traditional methods of classroom management usually disregard the importance of autonomy; nevertheless, the key is to motivate students to choose responsible behavior. When positive methods are in place, students will enthusiastically become responsible students. When students are not being coerced, they will cooperate and inhibit nonproductive behaviors. A primary reason coercive and consequence-based systems are ineffective is that they force students to suppress their autonomy. The alternative that we recommend is a positive motivation system that results in students choosing to cooperate with teachers. This simple and subtle difference is important to students' success. The viability of a system that gets students to choose schoolwork over play may seem implausible to many educators. Nevertheless, that is exactly what teachers must accomplish and the goal can only be accomplished when teachers address students' psychological factors.

When teachers abandon coercive techniques, students are more secure. In the classrooms we have described, students know and trust that they will not be subjected to psychological pain. They are confident the teacher will protect them from being belittled. As a result, they can effectively regulate their emotions, inhibit inappropriate behavior, and pursue their developmental potential. Every student can attain academic standards beyond usually expected levels. A classroom culture of excellence emerges when teachers use positive methods to motivate students.

To be successful using noncoercive methods, teachers must recognize the importance of creating success. When teachers are alert to the importance of students being successful in nearly every endeavor, they will find ways to create or generate success in many situations. Self-confidence is extremely important to students' success. However, educators will frequently overlook the fact that self-confidence is largely a result of students being successful. Teachers can influence student success by eliminating those variables that create self-doubt, cause emotional dysregulation, or diminish the chances of students' success. They will instead want to create a culture where all students work for the success of each student, and every student finds an open path to success. Teachers will need to use positive methods to motivate students voluntarily to pursue opportunities to excel. The best teachers we have known do not leave student success to chance or to be influenced by outside factors. Instead, they actively find ways to create success. Administrators promoting these methods must encourage and help teachers create success. They help and allow teachers to go out of their way to ensure every student's success. Administrators must notice when and how teachers generate success and describe the process to others.

Sometimes educators ask why we seem to ignore behavioral management research. Many of those studies have shown some effectiveness with methods that are much different from our own. We are familiar with most of those studies. However, nearly all such studies have shown very narrow results regarding particular behavior problems. We have little interest in whether an intervention can keep students from engaging in a few specific inappropriate behaviors while disregarding the overall impact on the class. Some of those studies did look at on-task rates associated with reinforcement systems. However, nearly all such studies used praise as the reinforcer for being on task; therefore, those studies played a role in developing our methods. Very rarely was any attention given to examining the side effects of the intervention procedure. We do not know of a single study that looked at the effects of intervention procedures on students' memory. Almost none of those studies investigated the effects of contingency systems on emotional regulation. Many professionals conducting those studies ignored emotion as a variable that could affect learning. However, we were looking beyond the behavioral management studies to develop a complete system for improving classroom instruction. We have little interest in techniques that do not contribute to remarkable academic accomplishments.

Instead education has mostly extrapolated from the studies to invent procedures that would be easier to use. In nearly every instance, those extrapolations misapplied the science on which those methods were founded. For example, timeout can be an effective intervention in certain circumstances when applied correctly. While timeout has been extensively used, most often it is not used correctly. Not only has education misapplied many techniques, but it has never evaluated the lack of success or the broader side effects.

Some may point out that very little research is available to support our methods. That is a fair observation and should be answered by the federal government. No other organization could hope to provide appropriate funding to evaluate systems for affecting change throughout schools. We would remind readers that much of the research on praise and differential social attention was conducted 50 or more years ago but seldom used. (See annotated bibliography.) What was not studied was how constant attempts to redirect inappropriate behavior or coerce appropriate behavior could derail the use of extensive praise. Research on the adverse effects of shaming students is also much more recent. Also, those who studied social reinforcers in the sixties and seventies did not understand the importance of the teacher-student relationship. The unified methods of interactive teaching are new.

The same question regarding research into teaching methods could be asked about all methods used in schools. If effective methods were being used throughout this nation's schools, all students would be at least reaching grade level criteria. Administrators should ask themselves two questions. First, how are their current methods working with all students, especially in the lower socioeconomic areas of their city? Secondly, when the original basic science is understood in detail, which methods are best supported? In effect, every school has evaluation data on the methods their teachers are using. If nearly all students are not reaching grade level criteria in academic areas, the methods are failing. Our experience is that no excuses, reasons, or explanations have any validity. The only variable that matters are the results with students and the appropriate methods used. This may be a hard reality to face, but if even a few dozen schools in this country will make a concerted effort to adopt our methods, all explanations for student failure will be pointless.

Equipped with the right interactive process, teachers can make a positive difference in the life of every student. While the process is not that difficult to learn, it is not widely known. By using this process teachers can have a positive influence on every aspect affecting the education of students. Only a few carefully selected interactions stand between students who disrupt the learning process for every student and students who cooperate with teachers. These carefully selected interactions are the difference between students who fail and students who at least meet minimum academic criteria for their grade level. Success every year with every student is within the reach of all elementary teachers. With the publication of this book, the obstacle is no longer the elusiveness of the methodology. The obstacle for teachers and administrators is to look past the years of institutional endorsement of current methods and see the possibilities of new methods. We, as educators, owe it to every student and to generations to come.

Sometimes in developing new skills, teachers are apparently successful, but forget how to use those skills before the next school year. This is because skills, including teaching skills, weaken over time. We have seen this happen several times over the years. Skills are more subject to a natural decline than information or knowledge, which is reasonably stable, especially if that knowledge is frequently used. However, even a professional baseball player who uses his skills of hitting, fielding, and throwing almost daily during the season, must practice them all several times per week or they will deteriorate. They have not forgotten how to play the game, but their skills can diminish. The same is true for all professional skills. The only solution is for a teacher or trainer to get back into the classrooms and encourage teachers to refresh their skills. Sometimes, especially during the first year or two of skill acquisition, this must be done a few times per year. However, the refresher training will be much easier than the original training.

Fortunately, the comparison to baseball does not continue forever. When teachers have effectively used the skills for a few years, they will seldom or never need refresher training. Cari has not had any additional training in interactive teaching in nearly 20 years. However, she has, on occasion, had to take a minute to think about what she needs to do better. One teacher in particular who worked for Art had to be reminded several times every year to renew her efforts in using the skills. She would invariably complain that the methods were not working anymore. Art and the teacher's direct supervisor could walk through the classroom and notice from student behavior that she had allowed her skills to slip. Eventually, all they had to do was remind her to renew her efforts in using differential social attention and she independently solved the problem in a few days.

In the first chapter, we described how students reach a level we called developmental actualization. Educators may question why they should care about a process that creates developmental actualization. That is a good question. The responsibility of education is to help students meet grade level criteria in academic areas and that is no small task. Developing actualization is not a standard for which schools are responsible. However, only a little over one-third of all students are meeting expected criteria by the end of eighth grade. Many methods and interventions have failed to solve the problem. That shortcoming is the reason for adopting the methods we describe.

Nevertheless, education has a problem of wider scope — schools cannot teach students everything students need to know. Current shortcomings in education have detracted from the fact that the need for knowledge and the ability to learn has expanded beyond what schools can accomplish. Fortunately, many students are learning beyond what schools teach by being around adults, older students, or listening to teachers. However, if schools want students to be able constantly to stay abreast of knowledge, they need to develop students who have the confidence and learning habits to educate themselves, at least in part. In the modern world, besides the immense amount of information available in printed materials we now have huge amounts of information at our fingertips via the internet. However, that means that besides teaching students to read, we must now teach them to distinguish between truth and fabricated information. The same holds true for visual information where TV news media often put their own spin on what they are reporting. Besides developing capable readers who are able to discern what should be believed, teachers must prepare students for various types of on-the-job training that will be required of them by employers.

In modern society, schools cannot hope to teach their students everything they need to know. To be successful schools must teach students to learn independently. That is a manageable task and students becoming accomplished learners is an achievable goal. The necessary elements to help students prepare for setting and achieving goals beyond the classroom are the necessary skills to learn and meet one's psychological needs. Developmental actualization is simply a result of those elements.

The methods we have described can produce remarkable results. However, to achieve those results teachers must execute the skills effectively. We have seen examples of teachers who have half-heartedly applied their new skills and subsequently complained that they do not work. A perfectly effective fire extinguisher, if used improperly, will not extinguish a fire. A perfectly tuned piano makes nothing but noise when played without skill. Unless they are applied correctly, the methods we teach are of little value.

To conclude this final chapter we will review the advantages of our methods. Teachers, principals, central office administrators, and state officials will find many reasons for adopting the methods we propose. As we have pointed out in previous chapters, schools are falling short of expectations in many areas. Some school districts and states have made modest progress over the last 20 years, but for the most part schools have little to show for their incredible efforts. Recent data show that math scores are continuing to slip and behavior problems persist.

Because of the problems in public schools, many parents are choosing home schooling or private school options. In recent years, home schooling has benefited from computerized instruction. We expect the number of parents choosing to home school their children will continue to increase; however, because many families have only one parent in the home or both parents working, we do not consider home schooling a threat to public schools.

Private schools are an option for some families and those schools could adopt noncoercive methods of teaching and help set the standards for other schools. However, private schools have less reason to change. Because most of their students are from affluent homes, they can reach minimum standards with traditional methods much like suburban schools. With more states adopting voucher programs, many states have more charter schools. The assumption, for 40 years, has been that making state money available to charter schools would increase competition and therefore improve all schools. We know of some charter schools that have done well, but increased competition will not benefit education, unless many alternative schools adopt noncoercive methods.

Of those who could benefit from our methods, the 60 million students in American public schools would benefit the most, and that is what inspired us to write this book. Students do not have a choice in the methods educators use; therefore, besides describing our methods we must convince educators that they should embrace noncoercive procedures. Unfortunately, convincing educators to change the way they teach is a far more formidable task than getting difficult students to excel. We have explained the benefits to students, but we have no way other than the strength of our words to motivate educators to admit that traditional methods are failing.

Traditional methods have evolved over the last 60 years, and just as interactions affect students, the necessity of defending those methods has influenced teachers. No educator adopted them intending to prevent learning, and, in theory, the contingency-based methods were plausible; therefore, American educators fully embraced the methods. However, as success with students continued to slip, teachers were assured the methods were sound, and erroneously concluded the problem was the students. As a result, more than a million elementary educators need to be convinced to abandon methods which they have defended thousands of times for new methods they have never seen used. Except for one thing, the task would be impossible; if even several hundred teachers, in a few hundred schools, would adopt noncoercive methods, nearly all teachers, in a matter of time, will demand the necessary training. Just as a successful culture in a classroom can influence a new student, the results in a few hundred elementary classrooms can convince every educator in the country. However, one factor complicates the issue. When only one teacher in a school is having exceptional results, other teachers resist the methods. Of the teachers in our examples, nearly all were the only teacher in their school using noncoercive methods. Each of these teachers faced the unenviable situation of colleagues not understanding or appreciating their methods. However, the situation is different at Art's school where every teacher understands and is committed to interactive teaching. They work together to help each other improve, and consider coercive techniques archaic. Although the children they work with are the most difficult students in the state, they know how to help them. For a given school to get most teachers to adopt noncoercive methods, we would estimate, initially, about four or five teachers would need to adopt the methods.

Since merit pay is nearly nonexistent, better academic results will not necessarily mean more pay for teachers; therefore, we must appeal to educators based on how interactive teaching benefits them in other ways. Higher achievement scores not only benefit the students, but teachers as well. As mentioned, teachers are under considerable pressure to get their achievement scores up. The best way for a teacher to avoid that pressure is to have the necessary methods to get nearly every student to meet grade level criteria. The only thing standing in the way of teachers and students reaching a mutual goal is a methodology that teaches students how to learn. We have found teachers know how to teach their subject matter, but struggle with getting students to become competent learners. Being able to listen, focus, and remember is one step to students reaching their goals. Getting students to reach grade level criteria is also dependent on their being able to work continuously. With interactive teaching, teachers can get students to function as a group where each student is helping every other student strive to excel.

Because principals are under considerable pressure to get achievement scores up, they will greatly appreciate the benefits of methods based on behavioral science and neuropsychology. Achievement scores and student behavior are the biggest challenges for most schools. Many schools have invested considerable time and money in helping teachers improve their teaching of curriculum areas. We believe that much of that training has improved instruction; however, schools have not realized a corresponding improvement in academic achievement. The reason is that students' ability to learn has not improved. Schools will not generate the expected improvement unless students become capable learners; even then teachers must eliminate the psychological stress that inhibits learning in many classrooms. Students disrupting classrooms also make a principal's job more difficult; unfortunately, many schools spend valuable time helping teachers respond to inappropriate behavior and considerable time is spent on behavioral IEPs. With the use of noncoercive methods, principals would have fewer students needing special education classrooms, and that would be especially true for behavior-disordered students. Also, the use of our methods will reduce the number of complaints from parents, and schools will have a lower turnover of students. We have noticed that when schools improve the school program, parents are reluctant to move and give up their child's school assignment.

District administrators also have reasons to promote the methods described in this book. They have put an immense amount of time and money into improving academic scores; unfortunately, many of those efforts have failed. Administrators also are under considerable pressure to contain costs, and interactive teaching can do just that. Most districts allocate significant amounts of money to special education classrooms. Because teachers who use noncoercive methods can successfully serve more difficult students, administrators would gradually need fewer special education classrooms. This would be especially true of programs for students with behavioral disorders and to a lesser extent for learning disabled students. These changes will not be easy; strong leadership will be necessary to overcome the inertia in many systems.

We suspect many administrators would prefer a system they could immediately implement throughout the district; however, no system that could produce the necessary change could be implemented in that manner. Instead, we suggest administrators encourage some principals and teachers to accept noncoercive methods. Teachers who do not believe in this methodology would not use it correctly, and as a result administrators would have a nearly impossible task of determining if the teacher or the methods were at fault. Art has found that teachers who believe in the methods work hard at learning the necessary skills and never try to sabotage results. We predict that school districts will soon enough find themselves needing to train teachers who want the skills; in most districts this could be done with no additional funds.

We have explained that the shortcomings in education are not the fault of students or teachers but the methods, and why these methods are failing. In addition, we described the skills necessary to set the course for a methodology revolution in American education. This is not a revolution to be feared, but embraced. We hope this book will serve to spark that revolution, guide the direction, and promote the advance of a new era in education. Moreover, we expect the current teachers in American schools to be the real heroes in carrying out this historic and necessary transformation. They will deserve hero status, because it will require hard work and remarkable courage to blaze the trail for noncoercive methods.

Annotated Bibliography

Aggleton, John P. (Ed.). *The Amygdala: A Functional Analysis.* Oxford, UK: Oxford University Press, 2000.
Used in medical schools but teachers can particularly benefit from chapters 6, 7, 15, and 18.

Astrup, Christian. *Pavlovian Psychiatry: A New Synthesis.* Springfield, Illinois: Charles C. Thomas Publisher, 1965.
Despite the psychiatric slant, this is the best book for teachers to understand the wide ranging influence of classical conditioning in the classroom.

Ayres, A. Jean. *Sensory Integration and the Child* (25th Anniversary Edition). Los Angeles, CA: Western Psychological Services, 2005.
Ms. Ayres was the pioneer in sensory integration and this is still a must read book in the field. In particular we draw attention to chapter 5 that describes how the sense of movement influences various areas of development.

Brandt, Kristie, B. D. Perry, S. Seligman, and E. Tronick (Eds.). *Infant and Early Childhood Mental Health: Core Concepts and Clinical Practice.* Arlington, VA: American Psychiatric Publishing, 2013.
This book in childhood mental health is important for all teachers. We specifically point teachers to three chapters, chapter 2 by Bruce Perry, chapter 8 by Nelson, Parker, and Siegel, and chapter 13 by Anzalone and Richey.

Bremner, J. Douglas. *Does Stress Damage the Brain?* New York: W.W. Norton, 2002.

A comprehensive book on the range of detrimental effects on the brain and mind. Educators cannot ignore this book.

Bremner, J. Douglas and M. Narayan. "The Effects of Stress on Memory and the Hippocampus Throughout the Life Cycle: Implication for Child Development and Aging." *Development and Psychopathology,* 1998. 10, 871–888.
Important study regarding the effects of stress on memory.

Collins, Marva and C. Tamarkin. *Marva Collins Way.* New York: Jeremy P. Tarcher/Putman, 1982.
This book makes a good case for being able to educate every child. She was successful with the most difficult students from the most difficult homes in the worst area of Chicago. Because she could do this 35 years ago, there are no longer any excuses.

Erikson, Erik. H. *Childhood and Society* (2nd ed.). New York: W.W. Norton & Company, 1963.
Erikson described the eight ages of man. These are all important to teachers, but in particular we drew on the first two ages that described the importance of trust and autonomy.

Gross, James J. (Ed.). *Handbook of Emotion Regulation.* New York: The Guilford Press, 2007.
The best book for understanding how the brain affects, controls, and fails to control emotion. Essential information for anyone attempting to influence the brains of other people.

Hopkins, B. L. and R. Conard. "Putting It All Together: Super School." In N. Haring and R. Schiefelbusch (Eds.) *Teaching Special Children.* New York: McGraw Hill, 1976 (pp. 342–405).
This evaluative research study was a forerunner of interactive teaching. The study demonstrated excellent academic progress in third grade classrooms. While struggling to find solutions in classrooms, educators have mostly ignored this study for 40 years.

Kaufman, Gershen. *The Psychology of Shame: Theory and Treatment of Shame-based Syndromes* (2nd. ed.). New York: Springer Publishing, 2004. (Originally published in 1989.)

In education we most often see the immediate effects of shame such as incomplete work, incorrect work, inadequate relationships with other students, and noncompliance. However, this is a definitive work that also describes the lifelong effects of shame.

Madsen, Charles H. Jr., W. C. Becker, and D. R. Thomas. "Rules, Praise and Ignoring: Elements of Elementary Classroom Control." *Journal of Applied Behavior Analysis*. 1968. 1, 139–150.

An early study that showed the importance of praise and ignoring.

Maslow, Abraham. *Hierarchy of Needs: A Theory of Human Motivation*. New York: Harper and Row, 1954.

The first psychologist to describe how human needs motivate human behavior.

Medina, John. *Brain Rules*. Seattle, WA: Pear Press, 2008.

In the first chapter the author makes a strong case for humans evolving and learning while in constant motion. However, chapter 8 explores stress, and chapter 9 sensory integration. Teachers will enjoy and benefit from reading this book.

Meyer, Urban. *Above the Line*. New York: Penguin Press, 2015.

This is a football book, but the first third of the book is the best description of leadership as it applies to forming a positive culture.

Neill, A. S. *Summerhill: A Radical Approach to Child Rearing*. New York: Hart Publishing Company, 1960.

There are two important aspects of this book that relate to *Freedom to Learn*. As early as 1921 Mr. Neill may have been the first educator to understand the importance of autonomy and self-discipline.

Perry, Bruce D. and J. Marcellus. "The Impact of Abuse and Neglect on the Developing Brain." Available on Scholastic.com.

Not a research article but this is a quick reference for teachers from a renowned author.

Perry, Bruce D. "Violence and Child: How Persisting Fear Can Alter the Developing Child's Brain." In D. Schetky and E. Bennedek (Eds.) *Textbook of Child and Adolescent Forensic Psychiatry*. Washington, DC: American Psychiatric Press Inc. 2001 (pp.221–238).

This chapter addresses some issues of the impact of fear on the developing brains.

Schein, Edgar H. *Organizational Culture and Leadership*. San Francisco: John Wiley & Sons, 2010.
   Written for business but is the best book on developing an organizational culture.

Sidman, Murray. *Coercion and Its Fallout*. Boston: Authors Cooperative, Inc., 2001.
   This book was first published in 1989 and is the definitive work on the disastrous effects of coercive methods.

Szalavitz, Maia and B. D. Perry. *Born for Love*. New York: William Morrow, 2010.
   This book not only describes the importance of relationships and empathy in human endeavors, but also describes how our modern culture stifles empathy.

Tangney, J. P., P. Wagner, C. Fletcher, and R. Gramzow. "Shamed Into Anger? The Relation of Shame and Guilt to Anger and Self-reported Aggression." *Journal of Personality and Social Psychology*. 1992. 62, (4) 669–675.
   Early study that examined the relationship of shame to anger.

Teicher, Martin H. "Scars That Will Not Heal: The Neurobiology of Child Abuse." *Scientific American*. 2002. 286, 3, 68–75.
   Essential work on the lasting effects of emotional and physical abuse.

Tronick, Ed. *The Neurobehavioral and Social-emotional Development of Infants and Children*. New York: W. W. Norton & Company, 2007.
   While this book is more focused on infant development, teachers should be aware of the work of Dr. Tronick on social-emotional development.

Watkins, Cathy L. "Follow Through: Why Didn't We?" *Effective School Practices*. Vol. 15, no. 1. (Available online.)
   Questions why educators more than 40 years ago ignored the research into effective methods of teaching.

Index

About the Authors

D R. ART WILLANS holds Bachelor and Master of Science degrees in education from Emporia State University and a Ph.D. in Developmental and Child Psychology from the University of Kansas. He has taught in the fields of education, special education, psychology, and child development, and administered several programs including a shelter for abused and neglected children and residential homes for behaviorally disordered children. He operates a preschool/ therapeutic preschool, where he has refined his revolutionary methods. Art and his wife live in Reno, NV, and during the summer can often be found hiking trails high above Lake Tahoe.

C ARI WILLIAMS is a teacher with a Bachelor of Science in Education and Special Education K-12, and an endorsement in Early Childhood/ Special Education from the University of Nevada, Reno. She met Dr. Willans when she interviewed for a position at his school and learned the basic methods in the book from him, while going on to make significant contributions to the methodology. Cari's professional experience includes serving as a Special Education Resource teacher for students from kindergarten through sixth grade, teaching Early Childhood Special Education, and currently teaching kindergarten. The concept for this book originated from her remarkable success in getting students to excel academically. Cari lives in Reno, NV, with her husband and three children.

A Note about the Publisher

New Society Publishers is an activist, solutions-oriented publisher focused on publishing books for a world of change. Our books offer tips, tools, and insights from leading experts in sustainable building, homesteading, climate change, environment, conscientious commerce, renewable energy, and more — positive solutions for troubled times.

We're proud to hold to the highest environmental and social standards of any publisher in North America. This is why some of our books might cost a little more. We think it's worth it!

• We print all our books in North America, never overseas
• All our books are printed on **100% post-consumer recycled paper**, processed chlorine free, with low-VOC vegetable-based inks (since 2002)
• Our corporate structure is an innovative employee shareholder agreement, so we're one-third employee-owned (since 2015)
• We're carbon-neutral (since 2006)
• We're certified as a B Corporation (since 2016)

At New Society Publishers, we care deeply about *what* we publish — but also about *how* we do business.

Download our catalogue at https://newsociety.com/Our-Catalog or for a printed copy please email info@newsocietypub.com or call 1-800-567-6772 ext 111

New Society Publishers
ENVIRONMENTAL BENEFITS STATEMENT

For every 5,000 books printed, New Society saves the following resources:[1]

24	Trees
2,188	Pounds of Solid Waste
2,408	Gallons of Water
3,140	Kilowatt Hours of Electricity
3,978	Pounds of Greenhouse Gases
17	Pounds of HAPs, VOCs, and AOX Combined
6	Cubic Yards of Landfill Space

[1]Environmental benefits are calculated based on research done by the Environmental Defense Fund and other members of the Paper Task Force who study the environmental impacts of the paper industry.

MIX
Paper from
responsible sources
FSC
www.fsc.org   FSC® C016245

new society
PUBLISHERS
www.newsociety.com